The Wonder Years

Parenting Preteens & Teens

The Wonder Years

DPI
DISCIPLESHIP
PUBLICATIONS
INTERNATIONAL

Sam & Geri Laing and
Elizabeth Laing Thompson

The Wonder Years

© 2001 by Discipleship Publications International

2 Sterling Road, Billerica, MA 01862

Printed in the United States of America

ISBN: 1-57782-159-9

Cover Design: Corey Fisher

Interior Design: Christine Nolan

To Sonny and Carolyn Sessions,
beloved directors of "The Swamp,"
the Atlanta Church of Christ's camp for kids,
for all they have done through the camp
and their ministry to inspire, mold and
save a generation of children.

Contents

Introduction

Sam

"Honey, could we please slow down?" I asked my daughter as we made our way down the aisle. She looked at me ever so briefly, nodded her agreement, and we continued on our way—too fast for me, too slow for her. As I looked down the corridor of smiling faces of our friends and family, I saw the young man who would soon replace me as the most significant male in my daughter's life. I felt my life moving at the speed of light to a destination for which I had prepared my daughter her whole life, but for which I could never completely prepare myself.

I think back now to my oldest daughter's childhood and try to remember...the sound of her voice when she was three, the look on her face at her fifth Christmas, her pigtails bouncing on her backpack as she walked down the driveway to board the bus on her first day of school, her joy at the births of her brothers and sister, her fearful first date, her senior prom, her departure for college, and the day I knew she was forever in love with the man of her dreams. I will never forget the angelic, womanly, frightened little-girl look on her face when I went into the bride's room to summon her on her wedding day. Even as I write these words, my mind is an impossible jumble of memories, images, thoughts and emotions.

I cannot remember everything nor can I stop time. I can only live my life in such a way as to help my daughter, and all of my children, to want to follow in my footsteps—footsteps that I try to direct in the ways of God. If I can do that, then I don't have to remember everything; I don't have to cling to the past. I don't have to hang my head in guilt, misery and despair because she is gone—because she is not. She is still in my life. She has a wonderful life with her new husband, and she has a spiritual life that is rock-solid and brimming with joy, hope, purity and promise for the future.

If I as a parent have this, I have everything. I still have my daughter. I know that wherever she is, whatever she is doing, she is doing well and is in good hands. Besides the salvation of my own soul and the joy of my marriage, there is no greater gift than this. If we can raise our children through the teen years and into young adulthood to a point that they are solidly on the right track, this will be one of the greatest and most crucial accomplishments of our lives.

Several years ago, Geri and I wrote a book about parenting titled *Raising Awesome Kids in Troubled Times.*[1] Our oldest, Elizabeth, was seventeen, David was fourteen, Jonathan was twelve and Alexandra was six. In that book we presented what we believed were the Biblical and common sense approaches that would help people to raise children who were not only good kids but faithful Christians as well.

Since that time, Elizabeth has graduated from high school and college and is married; David has graduated from high school and moved away to go to college; Jonathan has entered his senior year of high school, and Alexandra has become a teenager. Sometimes Geri and I look at each other with smiles on our faces and wonder how they, and we, have survived it all. The glorious thing is that the principles we wrote about really work. They have worked for us and for others, and they will work for you because they are timeless and have their origin in the mind of God.

Now we write again. This time, our aim is to help you as your children leave their innocence and enter the teen years. We write of *The Wonder Years*. How do you get your kids through the time when they are no longer little ones but are young people with souls for which they are accountable—but also with minds and emotions that are not yet ready for life on their own? It is one of the most difficult and challenging tasks you will ever undertake. Some of you are in the midst of it now, and you may doubt there is any hope for you and your kids. Some of you are about to embark on this new stage of life, and it scares you. Significantly, we write along with our daughter Elizabeth. Her insights will add immeasurably to the advice and wisdom we seek to impart.

I do not know how your children will turn out. I can only say that God loves them and has some things to teach you to help them and you go to heaven. We will once again share with you what we know of God's word and how it can help you navigate these treacherous but glorious years. We will once again share with you the experiences of raising our own four kids in the hopes that our less than perfect example can help you find your way through the fog and into the light. If these words and teachings aid you, then we are grateful that, in some way, we will have begun to repay the debt we owe to God for the immeasurable good that he has done in our lives.

NOTES

1. Sam and Geri Laing, *Raising Awesome Kids in Troubled Times*, (Billerica, Mass.: Discipleship Publications International, 1994).

1

Geri

I am once again reminded of just how desperately I need God. I have parented three children through the tumultuous adolescent years, and now I am starting with the fourth. Nothing has made me feel more inadequate and driven me more often to my knees than this task of guiding my children from the years of innocent childhood to accountable adulthood.

All of us who are parents of preteens or young teens find that the children we have loved, nurtured and trained have almost overnight become people we hardly recognize. They seem to be constantly "metamorphosing" before us: one minute the dependent and loving child, the next an unrecognizable adolescent; insecure yet knowing everything; desperately needing acceptance yet pushing us away; confused about everything but listening to no one.

As parents, we go through our own form of adolescence. We are faced with our own emotions, insecurities and fears. Just as we are beginning to have confidence that we can handle this role of "parent," all the rules change. We are forced to depend on God to take us to a new level as parents and even more so, depend on him to do for our children what we cannot do ourselves—guard them, protect them and move powerfully in their hearts and lives. During these years, we must take our walk with God to a deeper level than ever. In a very real and personal way he must become our strength, our source of wisdom, our hope and comfort.

God Is Our Strength

> The Lord is my strength and my shield;
>   my heart trusts in him, and I am helped.
> (Psalm 28:7a)

It is amazing how easily we can be lulled into complacency as disciples. We so quickly fall into the lifestyle of discipleship and lose the heart of devotion and passion for Jesus. If you have allowed yourself to become dead or dull spiritually, if you have lost your zeal and personal love for God, now is the time to change and rekindle the relationship. If you are merely a loyal church member, but you lack a life-changing, ever-growing relationship with God, do you really expect your children to choose your life above the exciting, attractive life that the world offers? We have seen far too many children of disciples choose the world over the dull, lifeless "Christianity" of their parents. Our children live with us every day, and they are the first ones to know if our walk with God is a doctrine to be followed or a genuine relationship to be savored. Some of us need to repent and renew our love for God.

For others of us, our reliance on God simply needs to deepen. Raising children is exhausting! Not only do they wear us out physically, but they can drain us emotionally. As our children have gotten older, life has gotten increasingly busy and more demanding. Many of us are raising not just one, but several children—each one with his or her own needs, demands and challenges. Add to this a job, household responsibilities, school, church and countless activities, and we go to bed exhausted and wake up feeling about the same. Sometimes we can feel like a mouse running on its treadmill and seemingly getting nowhere! I believe with all my heart that parents need God for physical and emotional strength. He can and does provide what we need. Hear his assurance to us in Isaiah 40:29-31:

> He gives strength to the weary
>   and increases the power of the weak.
> Even youths grow tired and weary,
>   and young men stumble and fall;
> but those who hope in the Lord
>   will renew their strength.

God Is Our Source of Wisdom

> If any of you lacks wisdom, he should ask God, who gives generously to all without finding fault, and it will be given to him. (James 1:5)

So many times as we raise our children, we honestly do not know what to do, what to say or how to answer. I believe one of the greatest gifts God has given us is the wisdom and advice of other disciples. I will be eternally grateful for the men and women

God has put in our lives to advise us and to help us at crucial times in the raising of our children. They have been instruments of God, saying exactly what we needed to hear, when we needed to hear it. However, it concerns me that so many of us turn to people for the wisdom we need to raise our children—even worldly, unspiritual advisors—before we turn to God. How much time have you spent praying for wisdom regarding the individual needs of your children? Many of us spend much more time worrying, fretting and agonizing over our children than we spend going to God in prayer for them! We miss sleep, we talk constantly to our spouses or our friends, and yet often our prayers to God are miniscule, mechanical and mundane.

As we write this book our youngest daughter is in the throes of the early teen years with all of its turbulence and turmoil. She is struggling with the decision to become a disciple and follow Jesus—not because we, her parents, are disciples or because her older siblings or even a number of her friends have made that decision, but because she wants to follow Jesus herself. The fight for her soul is on, and sometimes it seems that for every step forward, she takes two steps back. As a parent I fluctuate between wanting to protect her and being completely exasperated with her.

Well...what to do?! Recently, I spent an hour and a half walking for miles by myself praying to God. I prayed about many things but most of that time was spent praying for my youngest daughter and for God's wisdom to know how to raise her, what words to say to her, how to take her the rest of the way.

God has promised that he gives us that wisdom—not just a little bit of it—but a generous portion!

God Is Our Hope and Comfort

Why are you downcast, O my soul?
Why so disturbed within me?
Put your hope in God,
for I will yet praise him. (Psalm 42:5)

May your unfailing love be my comfort,
according to your promise to
your servant. (Psalm 119:76)

Years ago, when our children were very young I often took on decorating projects (and still do!) in our home. While Sam was out of town on speaking trips, I might refinish a piece of furniture, or I might paint or rearrange a room. He learned to be careful when he came home late at night—something might still be wet or "under construction" or moved. We always said that one of the reasons I enjoyed my projects was because it was one part of my life in which I could see a change in a short period of time. The children were young and required tremendous amounts of time and effort. And the results—the finished products—wouldn't be seen for eighteen years or more!

Preteens and teens are like a room that is in the midst of renovation. Even though the materials are all there, ready to put into place, there is a lot of work to do before the room is finished—and beautiful! We cannot become discouraged or faithless, especially when it seems like we have such a long way to go until we are "finished" and our children are what God wants them to be!

I've said it before but I must say it again: If there was ever a time for us to turn to God, if ever a time to trust in God, it is now, in the middle years of raising our children. The precious, adorable babies are gone, and yet we are so far from completing our jobs as parents. Prayer must be a very real part of our lives. The Bible must come alive to us as God's instruction book on how to live every day.

All of us have made mistakes along the way. Some of us have made terrible mistakes with devastating consequences. We must learn from our failures, repent of every sin we become aware of and trust in God. We must keep doing the things God wants us to do as parents, saying the things that are true and right and above all hoping in things that are yet unseen.

> We want each of you to show this same diligence to the very end, in order to make your hope sure. (Hebrews 6:11)

2

Sam

"Your sons do not walk in your ways."
1 Samuel 8:5

We are losing too many of our kids. They are choosing the ways of this world rather than the ways of God. As a minister and a leader, there is nothing more heartbreaking for me than to speak with a parent whose child has no interest in God's kingdom. In addressing this issue, I realize that I am dealing with feelings that run deep and with pain that is very real. It is not my intention to discourage you, but to alert you to the issues you must face if your children are to come into God's family and stay there. I suspect that some of you are desperate for help and others of you are out of touch with your real need. I pray that whatever your attitude, the challenges given in this chapter will encourage, enlighten and convict you.

What are the primary causes of children not entering the kingdom or leaving the kingdom after entering? There are many, but I will suggest seven.

1. Worldliness

> Do not love the world or anything in the
> world. If anyone loves the world, the love of
> the Father is not in him. For everything in
> the world—the cravings of sinful man, the
> lust of his eyes and the boasting of what he
> has and does—comes not from the Father
> but from the world. The world and its
> desires pass away, but the man who does the
> will of God lives forever. (1 John 2:15-17)

We live in times in which worldliness threatens
the church as never before. This sin is the single
greatest danger in the way of our children making it
to heaven. As this generation of disciples raises the
next, we must be vigilant that the love of the world
does not destroy our own love for God and our children's love for God as well.

How is worldliness affecting the way we raise our
children? Consider the following ways.

Obsession with academic performance. Success is
the goal worldly people have for their kids, and
grades are the primary vehicle to achieve it. Early
on, such parents begin worrying about what college
their kids will attend, the kind of job they will have,
and the income and prestige that will result. We
expect this kind of slavish idolatry from people in
the world, but not from the church. I must say with
shame, though, that some disciples are just as consumed with the worldly success of their children as
the most humanistic and materialistic people
around them. Others may not have gone to this
extreme, but are drifting dangerously from the values they had when they first became disciples. An

unrighteous ambition may destroy our souls and those of our children if we are not careful.

I am disappointed, dismayed and appalled at the unhealthy emphasis that some disciples are placing on academics. Not only are we pressuring our children, but we are also teaching them the wrong values. Were not Peter and John "unschooled, ordinary men" (Acts 4:13)? Did not Paul warn us of the dangers of human wisdom and relying upon our own intelligence (1 Corinthians 1 and 2)?

But shouldn't we do our best in everything we do? Shouldn't we strive for excellence? We should, both as a matter of discipleship and as a matter of character, but that does not mean that grades should become an obsessive focus. We should emphasize effort and hard work above grades. If a child has done his best, then we should be satisfied with the resultant grade. In some cases a B or a C is a tremendous accomplishment for which a student should be applauded. Academics come easier to some than others, and we must not make grades the primary judge of a child's performance or worth. When Geri and I receive our children's report cards, we are more concerned about their conduct evaluation than their academic grades. Conduct is more valued in the eyes of God, and we have found that when conduct evaluations are high, the grades take care of themselves.

Focus on athletic success. Athletic training and competition are excellent and needed activities in the lives of our preteens and teens, but they must be kept in proper perspective. Sports are valuable when we use them to teach our children to do their best and to work for a goal. Participating in athletics is a great way for our kids to get in shape, build confidence, socialize, learn how to handle defeat and victory, and discover the give and take of teamwork. And, at the end of it all, sports are just plain fun! But when we push our kids to be better than others and when sports become an obsession to win, we are on dangerous ground. Usually it is parents rather than kids who have the "win at all cost" attitude. We train this attitude into them—they just enjoy having a good time. Some of us, I fear, are reliving our childhood through our kids and are pushing them to have the glory we never had or to get glory for us now.

Overconcern with our children's possessions, appearance and style. It is a good thing to relate to our culture and society, but it is not good to focus on this to the point of becoming too concerned about appearances. Our children do not necessarily need to own every CD and video game, have a cell phone or possess all the latest electronic gadgets. Let us keep our children current in their dress and style, but let us also encourage them not to be slaves of current conventions.

Emphasis on leadership above servanthood. On one occasion the mother of James and John came to Jesus with a request (Matthew 20:20-28). She wanted her sons to sit with him in positions of prominence. Many of us are like her—we want our kids to be the superstars of the kingdom! There is a desperate need in our churches for young leaders, and God calls them to function at the highest level of leadership for which they have the ability. I realize we need more leaders, but how we define leadership is the pressing issue.

Many of us are more worldly than spiritual in our understanding of leadership and in our ambitions for our children. We train them to lead before we teach them to serve. What does this do to them? It corrupts their motivations. It makes them long for power and authority rather than service and sacrifice. It produces arrogance and conceit. It makes them come across cocky and brash rather than humble and sensitive. These attitudes are repugnant to God and will destroy our children's future in the kingdom.

Conceited, self-absorbed children must be humbled and broken. If not, they may be baptized because they want to be high-powered leaders or accomplish great goals, but not because they are grieved over their sins or long to serve God and others. Such children, if they do enter into the church, are worldly in their attitudes and offensive in manner. Most eventually fall away.

2. Unspiritual Parents

> Brothers, I could not address you as spiritual but as worldly—mere infants in Christ. I gave you milk, not solid food, for you were not yet ready for it. Indeed, you are still not ready. You are still worldly. For since there is jealousy and quarreling among you, are you not worldly? Are you not acting like mere men? (1 Corinthians 3:1-3)

Paul in this passage addresses those members of the church who still think and live like those who are in the world. He says that they are "worldly," and that they remain immature in their faith. The writer of Hebrews describes those who need to "go on to maturity" and grow up (Hebrews 5:11-6:1).

If one or both parents in a family are worldly, the kids are far less likely to become disciples. Your children go with you to church, they hear the sermons and lessons that you hear, and they can tell if you are making a sincere effort to live consistently with that teaching. They can tell if you are getting up early to read your Bible and pray, if you are making efforts to learn from other disciples, if you are humbly striving to grow and if you are sincerely reaching out to those who do not know the Lord. If they see this, they will forgive much! But if they see insincerity and a double standard, you will lose their respect, and they will develop a cynical attitude about spiritual things. The mumbled statement "I just don't want to be a disciple" most often comes from the mouths of children whose parents are not zealous, happy and loving disciples themselves.

Who we are at home is who we really are. If we are halfhearted or lukewarm, our children see it and do not want to follow in our footsteps. Why would they want to give their lives to something that is not worthy of their parents' best efforts? If they hear us complaining about how difficult it is to be a disciple, why would they want to inflict such a life upon themselves? If they hear Mom and Dad criticizing the church and running down other Christians, why would they want to be a part of such a fellowship? If your children are negative and critical toward the church, ask yourself if it is because of what they have seen in your life and heard from your lips.

3. Marriage Problems

It is virtually impossible to convert our children when our marriage is deeply troubled. I speak here of a marriage in which both partners are Christians. It is actually easier to convert a child when only one of the marriage partners is a disciple and there is a reasonably good marriage than when both are disciples, but the marriage is full of conflict.

Children long for their parents to love each other deeply. They want them to be happy, to get along and to treat each other respectfully. When this type of harmony is what they see, it shows them the profound difference between the church and the world. They hear the horror stories from their school friends about their parents' marriages, but if they see that their mom and dad are deeply in love, they are motivated and inspired to follow in their footsteps!

Some couples have been in the kingdom for years, but have never dealt with the problems in their marriages. They thought they could overlook these issues and just live with them, but now, they are reaping the bitter fruit of their sin as they see their kids unmotivated to become disciples. The fighting and arguing that their children have witnessed have damaged them deeply. They hear their parents' sarcastic tones and venomous words. They sense that their parents live more as roommates than as loving couples. None of us is perfect, and all marriages have their weaknesses, but if our children see that we are humble and sincere in trying to grow, they will extend us grace. On the other hand, if they see us ignoring problems or making excuses, they will not respect us or the church. It is time to get serious about making the changes in our marriages that we should have made long ago.

Geri and I once met with a couple who were having terrible difficulty with their oldest son. He was rebellious and angry, and it seemed that no discipline they tried could change him. We gave various suggestions, and at the end of our talk I happened to ask how their love life was going. The wife hung her head, and the husband flashed an angry scowl. Upon further questioning we found out that they rarely made love. The wife was "too busy" with her job and responsibilities, and the husband was frustrated, angry and tired of the continual feeling of rejection. We told them that their number one assignment was not their son, but their marriage. We challenged them to make time for an exciting, consistent love life. In a couple of weeks we received a jubilant phone call: the love life was back in place, the marriage was thriving and their son was making rapid improvement. When our children see that their parents are deeply in love and happy with each other, the odds of raising them to be obedient and respectful are greatly in our favor! (See chapter 4 for more on this topic.)

4. Weak Family Life

A family that is spiritual, close and happy produces godly children who want to follow in their parents' footsteps. Weak families, however, usually have spiritually indifferent kids. Even the most vibrant, loving teen group will have difficulty turning such kids around. Children from strong families, on the other hand, are usually converted even when the church and teen ministry are less than ideal.

To have a close family, there must be special times of sharing meals, fun and laughter. If a family rarely spends time together as a group, then the children will feel a sense of emptiness and disarray that can block them from the kingdom. Young teens from a close family are far less likely to be attracted to the world because they see in their home something greater than what the world has to offer. Why would children who have a loving, joyful family decide to go another route with their lives? Even in those cases where they decide to try another road, the chances are much greater that they will return when the family is a safe, fun and encouraging place to be.

Some of us need to radically change our priorities. We must stop being so concerned with our jobs and become more concerned with spending time with our families. Some fathers need to spend more time at home, even if it means a job change. The same is true for mothers. Some women cannot bear the pressures of holding down a job and being a nurturing, effective mom—this directly affects their families. There may need to be some financial sacrifices to keep Mom at home. Some mothers are going to have to trim back or change their hours or work from home in order to meet the needs of their families. Sometimes it is the husband who pushes his wife, against her better judgment, to continue in a bad work situation. The point is this: we must put our family's spiritual and emotional well-being ahead of financial or career considerations, and make any changes, no matter how radical, to build a healthy family.

Too long have we allowed ourselves to be swept along by the tides of this world. The feminist movement has identified many wrongs in society, but it has made a terrible mistake in telling women that their only way to self-worth is by getting a job, and that staying home to raise children is an unfulfilling choice. The Bible teaches otherwise. This worldly thinking has seeped into God's kingdom and hinders us in building warm, loving families.

5. Uninvolved Parents

Parents must invest themselves wholeheartedly in the lives of their children. To do less is to fail to love and care for them as we should. Some of us are devoted to making a living and keeping house, but are failing to give ourselves to our children on a heart level. We need to heed the advice of Peter who tells us to "love one another deeply, from the heart" (1 Peter 1:22b).

It takes intense effort to love our children in this way. It takes time, energy, thought and fervent prayer to be this kind of parent. I suppose some of us once thought that loving our children would be easy and would always be accompanied by emotions of warmth and affection. That is often true, but many times it is not, and we must decide to pour ourselves out to meet their needs when we may be feeling weary and unappreciated.

Children can tell when we are apathetic toward them. They can tell when we are emotionally detached. When we are always "too busy" it is another way of saying that we are selfish and do not love them as we should. As children enter into the preteen and teen years, they simultaneously become more perceptive and more difficult to love! Parenting will take more, not less, from us as they mature. Perhaps nothing will show our selfishness and weakness more than the challenge of raising our children. Too many times we try to employ the heavy hand of authority with preteens and teens whom we neglected in their earlier years. I am not saying this to discourage us from applying needed discipline, but to encourage us to repent of any past mistakes and step up our efforts to love our children right now.

6. Shaping Behavior Rather Than Molding the Heart

> Above all else, guard your heart,
> for it is the wellspring of life.
> (Proverbs 4:23)

God desires that we serve him with all our hearts. He does not want us to do what he says with a resentful, sullen spirit. Instead he wants us to obey out of love, trust and gratitude. It was the lack of wholeheartedness that caused God to be displeased with the children of Israel in the desert of Sinai (Numbers 14:20-24, 32:11-12; Deuteronomy 1:34-36). When Jesus criticized the Pharisees, it was because they were "going through the motions" but not having the right attitudes (Matthew 23:25-26).

Many of us have not imitated our heavenly Father in desiring heartfelt devotion in our children. We focus on getting them to do the right thing, but not on having the right heart. We wonder why we continually battle with them over the same issues— is it because we have not changed their hearts? Is it because we are satisfied with external conformity and not internal surrender? When I see parents arguing with a child or a child reluctantly going along with what his parents have said, my heart breaks. I know that one day the whole family will pay a terrible price for the mistake the parents are making. (I will provide more direction on training the heart in the next chapter.)

Many of us have low expectations for affecting our child's inmost attitudes, and so we do not try. Realize that the heart is where God deals with us, and efforts limited to shaping external behavior are doomed to failure. Sometimes we are too lazy and shallow to get down to that level. We prefer to have our children merely do what we say because it is more convenient and takes less energy. Raising children requires far more than programming them like a computer or training them by rote like a family pet.

7. Unresolved Issues and Attitudes

Training children means that we spend much time talking to them and teaching them. It means that we correct and help them to change many of their behaviors. If we are not careful, we can settle for "talking at" problems and issues rather than solving them. This produces a rebellious, exasperated child. One day this will catch up with us, and that day will probably be in the preteen or teen years.

Don't leave things simmering. Settle things. Bring discussions and arguments to a complete resolution. Get down to the heart of the matter and talk things out. Don't leave your child sullen and angry. Jesus perceived what people thought but did not say, drew those thoughts out and dealt with them. (See Matthew 9:1-8, Matthew 12:12-27, Mark 2:1-12, Mark 3:1-5, Mark 9:33-37.) Imitate Jesus. Gently draw out what your children are feeling and thinking. The writer of Proverbs wisely reminds us,

> The purposes of a man's heart are
> deep waters,
> but a man of understanding draws
> them out. (Proverbs 20:5)

As you draw out and discuss their thoughts, pray for wisdom and do your best to apply the appropriate scriptures. Get advice afterwards for other scriptures that would apply. Keep talking until you understand and agree with each other, even if it takes several sessions. Get someone else to help you if you are unable to come to closure. Only when things are resolved have you done your job as a parent.

The result will be that your children, unlike so many others, will have hearts that are free of bitterness and frustration. There will be no lingering anger or no smoldering resentments to hinder their relationship with God or with you. Our families will reap the reward of peace that David promised us long ago:

> How good and pleasant it is
> when brothers live together in unity!
> (Psalm 133:1)

∿

I have tried in this chapter to identify the main reasons we fail to help our kids come into the kingdom. I realize that this could be a discouraging and negative chapter. I hope it is neither. Instead, I hope that it helps you to identify areas in which you need to change. I hope that you will be determined to take action and make efforts to overcome any weaknesses rather than being defeated by them.

Some of you reading this book started your journey as disciples at a much later time in life than others have. If so, you may be desperately trying to show your preteen or teenage children that your new life is great and is the way that they, too, should live. Hopefully your children will see your radical changes and newfound joy and will want to follow Jesus as you have. However, the longer you have waited to make your decision, the greater your challenge may be. I want to encourage you to try with all of your heart to reach your children, with the hope that they will respond to the good news that you have found.

The patterns of your past may be hard to overcome, and the results in the lives of your children may already be very serious. Do not be overwhelmed with guilt and regret, but be grateful for the salvation that has been given you. Let your joy and love shine forth, and be patient.

In our congregation and in families all over the world there are examples of moms and dads who became disciples when their kids were older, and who finally reached them for the Lord.

Just a few weeks ago, we saw a father and mother in our church baptize their oldest daughter. Their marriage was a disaster, and their family was in despair when they came to the church four years ago. Even after becoming disciples, they made many mistakes, had much to learn and many difficult changes to make. They stuck with it, humbly pressing forward in spite of all the obstacles.

Their daughter, who had been virtually stone-faced during the first few years they were in the church, finally began to soften. It was amazing to see God open her heart just as he did for Lydia (Acts 16:14). As they tearfully joined together in baptizing her, other parents in the congregation took heart. So may you, too, be inspired.

Never give up, always hope, keep on praying. With God, all things are possible, and one day, the prodigal may come home!

The Heart of the Matter

3

Sam

God has always been more concerned with the inside than the outside. Jesus said it this way: "First clean the inside of the cup and dish, and then the outside also will be clean" (Matthew 23:26). Jesus understood the human tendency to be more concerned with making a good impression than with being righteous. If this is a challenge for adults, then with preteens and teens it is a mega-challenge.

The teen world is all about appearance and performance. It is about acceptance and conformity. Grades, athletic ability, popularity, clothes, talking the right talk—all of these are the standards with which their peers judge our preteens and teens, and often judge them unmercifully.

If your children are going to become disciples of Jesus, they must learn to think differently—completely differently—than the world around them. This is no small task and will be perhaps the greatest challenge you face in raising your children.

Perhaps the place for you to begin is with yourself. How do you evaluate your children? What is important to you? If you are more concerned with their grades, athletics and worldly achievements, then you could be the major cause of their spiritual downfall. Ask yourself, and answer honestly, what are the things that most matter to you? What gets you the most upset and disappointed with your kids? Is it when they make a bad grade or struggle in sports?

We may mask our attitudes under the guise of saying we simply want our kids to excel for the glory of God, but is it really all about our own pride and worldliness? Such children are highly unlikely to become true disciples. As we established in chapter 2, the first thing some of us need to do is to repent of our own worldliness before we can think about helping our children to overcome theirs.

God is a father who looks at the heart above performance and appearance. This is the way he looked at the young shepherd boy David. His older brothers were bigger, stronger and more outwardly impressive than he was, but God looked at something far more important—the heart. Concerning David's brother Eliab, God said to Samuel, "Do not consider his appearance or his height, for I have rejected him. The Lord does not look at the things man looks at. Man looks at the outward appearance, but the Lord looks at the heart" (1 Samuel 16:7). It was David's heart for God and desire for integrity that caused God to select him to be the next king of the nation of Israel.

DEFINING HEART

Heart is more important than any other quality we possess. Solomon advises,

> Above all else, guard your heart,
>   for it is the wellspring of life."
> (Proverbs 4:23)

Jesus said,

> Blessed are the pure in heart,
>   for they will see God. (Matthew 5:8)

But what does it mean to have "heart"? How do we define it? Let's consider several essential elements.

1. A Sense of Need

The most fundamental quality of heart is knowing our need for God. Within the heart of preteens or teenagers there must be a hunger and thirst for God himself. They must sense in their deepest souls an incompleteness and emptiness apart from God, a void that God alone can fill. It is this profound sense of loneliness apart from God that will drive your young ones to their knees in a desperate search to find the fulfillment that God alone can bring them.

All of your teaching and influence must be directed towards helping them to see and feel this need. In all of your conversations and prayers this must be your greatest desire for them—to have a hunger and thirst for God that will motivate them to never be satisfied until they have given him their lives.

2. A Fear of God

In his magnificent book written to direct the paths of young people, Solomon says, "The fear of the Lord is the beginning of knowledge" (Proverbs 1:7a). The place to start is having a tremendous sense of the awesome glory of God. Our children must have a proper fear of God within their hearts before they will ever find their way to salvation. Too many kids raised in the church fail to have a proper sense of the holiness and righteousness of God. While they have grown up praying to God and believing that he loves them, they must come to the point of realizing that they are separated from God because of his righteousness and because of their own sins.

Before they can know grace and mercy, they must come to know righteousness, holiness and judgment. They must learn that God must be approached with reverence and awe (Hebrews 12:28) and that it is "a dreadful thing to fall into the hands of the living God" (Hebrews 10:31). All too often we want to teach our children the great love of God before they have learned the costliness of that love. Before they can understand the cross, they must understand that it was their sin that made it necessary. The cross was not only a demonstration of God's wonderful love, but a display of his judgment against their sin.

Some teens are not motivated to become disciples because they have no fear of God. Becoming a disciple, to them is just another option—just as it is an option to select certain classes, social clubs or activities at school. Why would one want to become a disciple, with the tremendous challenges involved, if it is simply one of many other alternatives? If there is no awe of God or fear of judgment, teens will never have the profound conviction and zeal that are required of them to become followers of Jesus.

3. A Tender Conscience

Paul told the young man Timothy of the need for a good conscience (1 Timothy 1:5). The development of a good conscience in the life of a preteen or teen is paramount. The conscience is an inner compass God gives us by which we judge ourselves. Our conscience serves as judge and jury for our conduct, thoughts and actions. The development of a strong and righteous conscience in our children is one of the most important jobs we have as parents. Do you want to raise children who will turn out great and who will one day follow God? Then raise them with a conscience that is easily convicted when it has done wrong and that cannot be satisfied until all things in life are put right with God. To build this into our children, we will need to share with them our own struggle with sin and our own efforts to have a clear conscience. There are no easy answers. It will take prayer and consistent application of the Scriptures.

4. Righteous Convictions

When the young teenager Joseph (Genesis 39) found himself away from his family and challenged with the temptation of an easy sexual exploit, his convictions were tested. Teens show their true colors when they are away from the influence of their families and out on their own. Those who conform to the thinking and actions of their "group," show that they do not have righteous convictions. Joseph is a great example to them of one who did not give in to the pressure brought upon him. He stood up to the temptation because of his beliefs about right and wrong: "How then could I do such a wicked thing and sin against God?" (Genesis 39:9b). Do you know how your teen would respond? As a parent you must lead and teach and pray so that your children will have a conviction about right and wrong that will cause them to stand up for what is right—regardless of the pressures and temptations.

However, if your children fail such a test, the worst thing you can do is to give up on them. You must be careful not to let your personal feelings of disappointment take precedence over the need to help your children. Let the experience of failure be one that helps you, and them, see what was lacking. Help them pick up the pieces, get up and try again.

5. Love for God

Jesus said that the greatest commandment was to "love the Lord your God with all your heart and with all your soul and with all your mind" (Matthew 22:37). Our children must ultimately come to a point where they have a personal love and devotion to God himself. Nothing else will do. Their love for God must be greater than their love for the world, their families or anything else. So often young people think that becoming a disciple simply means joining the church and becoming a part of the teen ministry rather than loving God and having a relationship with him. The next section will provide some needed guidance in this crucial area.

DEVELOPING HEART

How can we help our kids develop a heart for God? Let me give some practical suggestions.

1. Prayer

As your children mature, you must wisely guide them into a deeper and more personal life of prayer. They must learn to converse with God on an intimate and heartfelt level. To do this they will need to have regular quiet times in the mornings, imitating the example of Jesus who spent his early mornings in prayer (Mark 1:35). They must learn to pray to God on their own. While it may be a good idea to occasionally have quiet times with teens to help them get started, it is not wise for parents to continue this practice for long. Teens, like adults, must learn to be close to God on their own.

2. Longer times with God

As kids get older they need to occasionally take additional time for prayer over and above their usual quiet times. I suggest that they go out on a Saturday or Sunday morning when they have more time to be alone with God in prayer. The early starting time of schools precludes lengthy quiet times for teenagers on weekdays. This means that for them to have any sort of an extended prayer life, they will have to take advantage of holidays and weekends. I urged my sons David and Jonathan in this direction during their pressure-filled high school years. When I sensed that their spiritual lives were becoming stale and that their schedules were becoming stressful, I encouraged them to go out for longer quiet times on Saturdays. They have both told me how this has helped them, and I have seen the dramatic results in their transformed attitudes afterwards.

3. Time Outdoors

The men and women of the Bible, unlike us moderns, spent a great deal of time outdoors. God has created an amazing and beautiful world, and we cheat our children and ourselves if we never get outside and enjoy it. When our children were studying to become disciples, we frequently urged them to go outside and spend time in nature alone with God. We urged them to be with God and enjoy the beautiful blue sky and to observe the glorious beauty of nature all around them. We urged them to contemplate the greatness, wisdom, intelligence and awesome power of God that they could see in his world. This enabled them to think more clearly and to learn to enjoy God's presence in a deeply personal way.

Both of my sons have a unique love for nature. David found a beautiful lake on his college campus, and it has become his special place to draw near to God. Whenever he comes home, he always goes out to a lake near our house to pray. Recently when he brought home a young man whom he had helped to become a disciple, he took him out to the same place, and they prayed there together. My son Jonathan often will get on his mountain bike and be gone for hours on a Saturday when he senses that he needs more time to be with his Father. I taught my boys about drawing close to God in nature as a result of my own experience and my observation of the heroes of faith in the Bible. This has helped them to be young men who are genuine and real and not simply products of the influence of others.

4. Wrestling in Bible Study

Teach your kids to open their Bibles and work hard to find out what passages mean to them. As parents we often try to do too much for our children rather than challenging them to "work out [their] salvation with fear and trembling" (Philippians 2:12b). There is nothing quite like the experience that comes from having a passage in the Bible jump out at us in a moment of insight. We can spend so much time trying to answer their questions that we do not urge them to go into their rooms, open their Bibles and work it out for themselves. We know that teens are developing heart and character when they come back to us and share the insights into the Scriptures that God is giving them on their own.

5. Keeping a Journal

Teach your teens to write down their thoughts, feelings, insights and observations in their own personal journals. This will enable them to begin to wrestle through their faith and come up with their own convictions. Our children hear many sermons and receive a great deal of discipling and feedback; they must begin to process this information on their own. The young person who is praying, reading and being discipled can often become overwhelmed, confused and frustrated. But kids who write things down and work them out will begin to learn lessons and develop personal convictions.

There is no easy way to teach your kids to have convictions. In fact the first step is to have convictions of your own and be a person of genuine spirituality yourself. If your child is failing to develop convictions and character, look within yourself and see if you are just going through the motions. Check out your own motivations—do you want your child to do well just to make you look good? It is easier to cleanse the outside of the cup than to deal with the inside...both in ourselves and in our children. But when we expect of ourselves the proper attitudes of heart and conviction, we have the best chance of producing those same convictions within our kids—convictions that will bring them into the kingdom and keep them there for life.

Two Are Better Than One

4

Sam

Two are better than one,
    because they have a good return
        for their work:
If one falls down,
    his friend can help him up.
But pity the man who falls
    and has no one to help him up!
Also, if two lie down together, they will
        keep warm.
    But how can one keep warm alone?
Though one may be overpowered,
    two can defend themselves.
A cord of three strands is not quickly
        broken.
                    Ecclesiastes 4:9-12

Do two walk together
    unless they have agreed to do so?
                    Amos 3:3

The most important factor in raising your children is your relationship with God. The condition of

your marriage is next, hands down. It takes two of you to get the job done. You have different roles, personalities, strengths and talents—both of you are equally needed. In the great wisdom of God, he has placed you together as a team to carry out one of the greatest and most challenging works of your life.

Children reflect their parents' marriage. They observe it, they feel it, they take part in it, and the very fabric of their character is shaped by it. They are the transmitters of your marriage to the outside world. Behold a sunny, warm child who is adjusted to authority and to life. Look at his parents, and you will probably see a loving and peaceful marriage. Observe a child that is sullen, angry, discouraged and withdrawn. If you look closer, you will in all likelihood discover a marriage afflicted by distance, deadness and hostility.

As children mature, they become more aware of the world around them and especially of their parents' world. They are not as naive as we think. They hear the words we speak, even when we think they are not listening. They feel the distance and anger between us; they hurt when they sense a deadening of our love. They secretly fear that we might break up, leaving them as victims of the plague of divorce that stalks our land. They see the hurt and longing in the eyes of their unloved and lonely mother. They feel the pain of their father's soul that longs for the respect and friendship his wife denies him.

If you have a weak marriage, do you really believe you can go on as you are, with a marriage that needs to be healed, that needs to grow, to change, to blossom? Do you think you can carry on with this sickness under your roof and not infect your children? Do you maintain that God's plan is for you to trudge your way through life with a burdened marriage? Do you think that God's promises of growth, release and freedom are not really true? Do you not know that the relationship your children rely on most to reveal to them God's great love is their parents' marriage?

If you are in a difficult marriage, get help. There is always hope, and there is always a way to change. When Geri and I authored *Friends and Lovers*,[1] the unshakable conviction we articulated as the thesis of the book was, "Any two people can change. Any marriage can be fixed. Any marriage can become great." We believed it then, we believe it today. We have seen too much proof to doubt it. Go back and read the book, and put the principles to work in your marriage. Get help in your local church. If they are unable to help, ask them to put you in touch with more experienced counselors in another congregation. Not only are your souls at stake, but the souls of your children as well.

Please remember the following truths:
- A godly, loving marriage is the foundation upon which you raise your children.
- Fix your marriage before you try to fix your kids.
- Maintain a loving, happy marriage; do not neglect it to devote yourself to the children.
- Take whatever steps needed to heal and strengthen your marriage; do not be satisfied until you are on firm footing.

Benefits of a Healthy Marriage

A good marriage is a powerful bulwark, protecting your preteens and teens from being drawn into sexual sin. Wherever they turn, our kids are confronted with sex and sensuality. While we need to protect them as much as possible from the world's influence, we cannot shield them forever. They must face the temptations of the world, and they must see through them in order to overcome them. Satan will present immorality as the best way, the fun way, the exciting way to have a great sexual life. He will present chastity, purity and monogamy as the ultimate route to boredom and dullness. What are we to do?

The best antidote to this poison is the daily exposure of our children to a marriage that they can plainly see is exciting and fulfilling—one that brings their parents, and them, all the joy that they can imagine. It is in this way we "overcome evil with good" (Romans 12:21). When Elizabeth was in high school I remember her saying, "I want to marry a man who looks at me the way that Dad looks at Mom." Elizabeth knew why and how I so greatly love and respect Geri. She knew that the love and attraction she saw in my eyes for her mother were what she wanted from her future husband, and one day could have if she would build her life and marriage on the same foundation. It would have been virtually impossible for her to be drawn away from God's kingdom by a young man, no matter how impressive, who tried to persuade her to compromise her sexual morals.

Children will grow up to imitate the love and respect they see between their mom and dad. For the most part, a peaceful marriage makes for peaceful relations between everyone else in the house. A marriage marred by conflict, separation and sullen silence replicates itself into the family as well,

You will have to team up with your spouse if you want to navigate your kids successfully through the wonder years. If you don't, you could lose them. Draw wisdom from one another. "Many advisers make victory sure," said Solomon (Proverbs 11:14). Why do we not turn to the wisdom of the counselor we married? When issues arise that are difficult, it will take both of you to figure it out. Each one of you has blind spots. Alone you will lose objectivity; by yourself you will be stumped. Teamwork can save the day, and your children as well.

I cannot say how many times Geri has saved me, and I her, from making mistakes in raising the kids, especially in their teen years. Both of us have our individual strengths in parenting and our particular insights into each of our children. Geri has a woman's and a mother's intuition; I have a man's and father's strength and firmness. Geri often sees what I do not, and she kindly lets me know when one of the children needs more of my time, attention and love. I can see when Geri is becoming overwhelmed and anxious, and I can step in and calm her fears and give her some relief from the burdens she bears.

When the emotional load becomes too heavy for either one of us, we help each other. When Geri is becoming frazzled with the duties and load of her work, it can show up in fretting and shortness with the kids. It is then that I step in and take off some of the pressure. I help directly with her work, or I let her know that a task is not really that urgent, or I just invest more personal time with the children so that she knows she is not alone in her concerns. Geri helps me to see when I become distant, abrupt and negative. She lets me know if I have hurt anyone's feelings, and if they need some fatherly reassurance and forgiveness.

We have a rule that has served us well: "Both of us cannot have a bad attitude at the same time." Bad attitudes are never good, mind you, but they are devastating to a family when both Mom and Dad go down together. Don't let it happen. If your spouse is struggling, keep your attitude faithful and spiritual. If you do, you will help him or her repent and repent quickly.

Work out disciplinary matters together. As children mature, your methods of discipline must also. These decisions will require great wisdom, and more than ever you will need to consult each other. In fact, you should never make a major disciplinary move without consulting your spouse, and without his or her agreement and support. It is most harmful for parents to disagree in areas of discipline. Never disagree with each other over matters of discipline in front of the kids. If you think your partner has made a mistake, calmly and humbly call for a private discussion. Work it out together, and then present a united front. Some parents have a running battle about discipline; one thinks the other is too hard or too weak. This must be resolved. I have seen this kind of disagreement cripple parents, ruin children and wreck marriages. If you cannot work it out in private conversations, then go to the wisest counselors you can find. Do not rest until you have a clear understanding of the direction you need to take.

Let me summarize some of the practical teachings of this chapter:

- Consult each other about the kids. Continually discuss what each of you sees in them, what they are working to change, how they are doing, and what they need from each of you.
- Give each other constructive criticism and helpful advice. Do not do this in a negative and fault-finding way, but as teammates who have the same goal. Get help and advice from wise spiritual counselors.
- Relieve one another when you see that the emotional, spiritual, mental and physical toll is overwhelming for your spouse.
- Work out disciplinary issues together. Do not act independently of each another. Do not disagree in front of the kids, and if you cannot agree, get help from others.

We opened this chapter with a verse that says, "Two are better than one." Believe it! Next to your relationship with God, your marriage is your most important resource to see your kids safely through the wonder years. Cultivate and rekindle your love, friendship and closeness with each other. Work together as a team. The very act of cooperating in raising the kids can be a powerful source of bonding between husband and wife. And then, one day, when they are out of your home, married and still in God's kingdom, you can know that together you accomplished one of the greatest achievements of your lives.

NOTES

1. Sam and Geri Laing, *Friends and Lovers* (Billerica, Mass.: Discipleship Publications International, 1996).

Father and Son

5

Sam

> My son, give me your heart
> and let your eyes keep to my ways.
> Proverbs 23:26

One of the great tragedies of life is the failure of fathers to be close to their sons. No matter where you go, the story is the same: fathers and sons are distant from one another. Time after time as I have addressed this problem in sermons and lessons, men have come up to me afterwards with pain in their hearts and tears in their eyes. They admit their failure to be bonded with their fathers and the difficulty they have in building close relationships with their sons. Why this is so, I will not address. What I will address is the crying need to change it and how practically to do that. We live in a time of crisis in male identity. Men do not know how to be men. They seem lost between the extremes of ineffective weakness and prideful posturing. A large part of the reason is that no one has taught them how. Young boys are left virtually alone to raise themselves and to figure out the immense challenges they face as they grow into manhood. Mothers try, and try mightily, but they are not men; try though they may, there are some things that only a man can teach a boy. The role of the father is essential in a young man's life.

What should a father provide for his son? In answer to that question, consider the following qualities:

1. Closeness

A father should be comfortably close to his son and free to talk to him about anything. He should be bonded to his son in heart. In the verse that begins this chapter, Solomon appealed to his son to give him his heart. I believe every father will have to make this appeal throughout his son's life if they are to be deeply bonded. Something inside young men causes them to want to drift away, to live in their own world, to be loners, to be independent. To have a relationship, fathers, you cannot wait on him to come to you, you need to make the first move. Do not sit back. Love the way God loved you: love first, reach out first, reach out repeatedly, never give up—even when you grow weary. Give of yourself until your son knows and trusts that you love him, and he will love you in return.

Give him your time. Time with him alone. Time to talk, time to play, time to do things—jobs that need to be done around the house, things he likes to do, things you can do together. For a young man, time means love. It means you care enough to give him yourself. It is the only way. Without it, your relationship will never grow.

Give him your attention. Listen. Hear what he has to say, and hear how he says it. If you listen carefully enough, you will hear the thoughts of his inmost heart.

Give him your affection. A boy needs his father's manly embrace, his pat on the back, his masculine kiss on the cheek.

Give him your emotions. Let your guard down. Let him see you cry. Let him see your feelings of sorrow, your emotions of love for him. So many times we want to do this, but hold back. The reasons are rooted in selfishness, pride and fear. Those of us who have lost our fathers regret all the things we should have said to them before they were gone, right? Do not let that regret find its way back into your life again; pour out your feelings to your son. Do it with the spoken word, and if that is difficult for you, write it down and let him keep it forever as a remembrance of your heart. Fathers who do this can win the hearts of their sons and can lead their sons to have a relationship with God.

2. Confidence

Perhaps the greatest sign of a father's good influence is in the level of confidence displayed by his son. All young men need the approval of their fathers, and they are empty, discouraged and rebellious without it. A father's belief in his son is, I believe, the single most important factor in building his son's sense of peace and joy in life. If your son is not confident, look and see if you have done all you can to communicate your love for him and belief in him.

Give him your encouragement. Let him know all the things you love and respect about him. Tell him when he has done well. Do not reserve your observations to pointing out his many failures and mistakes. That is what boyhood is about—making mistakes, and making plenty of them.

It helps your son if you let him in on the mistakes and failures from your younger days. It lets him know he is not alone in his feelings of embarrassment and awkwardness, and that he can get through them just like you did. You will find that instead of making your son lose respect for you, your openness will make him feel closer to you.

3. Masculinity

One the greatest gifts you can give your son is to teach him how to be masculine, how to be manly. It has always been difficult to know how to be a man, and in today's world it seems more difficult than ever. Masculinity and manhood have been assailed on every side. Young boys need a powerful and healthy role model to follow if they are to navigate their way through these treacherous waters and become strong men.

Help your son find his way into the world of sports. While every young boy does not have to be an outstanding athlete in order to be manly, he does need to be able to be comfortable in the world of play that is the common domain of young boys. If he holds back because he is not naturally talented or is disinterested, it will limit and damage his development. Do not let your son surrender his involvement with other boys just because it is easier for him to avoid this challenge. Do not let him retreat into the world of loneliness, video games or femininity. Urge him to venture out and relate to the other young men around him. I am not saying that you should pressure your son to be someone he is not; some boys are more interested in other pursuits. You simply need to help him be well rounded.

Help him to understand his sexuality and to develop a healthy attitude about it. As your son enters the teen years, he will need much help from his father about sexual issues. You are the one to give him "the talk" about sex. You are the one to help him understand his awakening sexual desires. A young man who is striving to live righteously will often be plagued with guilt and uncertainty concerning sexual temptation and will need quite a few talks with his dad to sort things out. I refer you to the chapter on purity in my book *Mighty Man of God*[1] in which there is a lengthy section explaining the difference between lust and sexual temptation. I have had many of these talks with my own sons, helping them to know when their interest was innocent and when it crossed the line to sinful lust.

Help your son stay away from the plague of masturbation. Sex was created by God to be enjoyed in the marriage relationship, as an act of love and communion with our wives. Masturbation takes sex out of the realm of married love and places it in the realm of personal gratification. Masturbation is enslaving, fills young men with guilt and robs them of their confidence. It leads to lust and fantasies and a secret life. As a father, help your son to learn the manly practice of self-control and to save his sexual experiences for marriage.

Your son's close relationship with you is the best defense against homosexuality. This horrible sin is now making tremendous headway into the very core of our culture. Your son hears every day at school and in the media how some people are "just born that way." He may begin to doubt his own sexuality, and there are those who will try to convince him that he is indeed a homosexual. Since the Bible teaches that homosexuality is unnatural (Romans 1:26-27) we need to have our own convictions very deeply grounded and know that no young boy, including your son, was made this way.

4. Manners

We live in a world that is becoming increasingly rude and ill-mannered. Young men seem to be leading the way. Fathers, teach your sons to be gentlemen. Teach them to be courteous and kind to others. Teach them to pull themselves up out of self-absorption long enough to see the needs and to consider the feelings of others. Teach them to smile warmly and give friendly greetings to those they meet. Teach them to respond with more than grunts and groans when they are asked a question. Teach them to make eye contact and show interest when they meet people. You need to especially teach them to be courteous to women. Teach them to open doors for women, to carry their books, to give up their seats for them, to carry their packages for them, to show deference to them in every social situation. If your son does this, he will never be without female admirers, and he will one day marry a wonderful young woman!

5. Humility

Confident doesn't mean cocky. Is there anything more offensive than a cocky young man? Some young men, in the attempt to appear confident, act like know-it-alls. This only makes them look foolish to other people, with the possible exception of other young men who are playing the same game. Teach your son to respect authority and to respect others, especially older people. Humility begins with the way he treats you and his mother. It continues with the way he speaks to his own brothers and sisters at home. The sneering "I'm better than you" attitude that is so prevalent among young men must not be allowed to become part of your son's character.

Once I was speaking with a man after a performance when his preteen son came up. "Dad can we go now?" the boy said with a whiney, moaning, "I'm more important than the rest of the world" attitude. His father sent him away saying, "Son, we will leave in just a few minutes; just be patient." The boy sulked off with a scowl on his face. This father failed to deal with his son's cocky, prideful attitude. Believe me, such an attitude may one day keep that young man out of the kingdom of heaven unless it is faced and dealt with!

Some of you fathers reading this have sons who have much stronger personalities than yours. If this is the case, you will have to become a stronger man if you are to successfully raise your son. A strong-willed boy with a soft-spoken father will become increasingly rebellious and angry as he matures unless his father deals firmly with him. Some of you men are going to have to become more powerful in manner. It may seem unnatural to you; it may not be the way you needed to be dealt with at your son's age, but it is the way your son needs to be dealt with. If Paul was willing to "become all things to all men" to save as many as possible, then some of us are going to have to do the same in order to save our own sons.

I recently had a discussion with a father whose twelve-year-old son was drifting further and further away from the church and from his family. His behavior in school was becoming increasingly worldly and arrogant. The father just did not want to believe this about his son and was so easygoing that he didn't even see it. I had a very forthright discussion with him about his son, and I challenged him to become a stronger and more forceful personality in leading his son. I even offered to have this talk with his son myself.

The father quickly grasped what I was saying and said, "No, this is something I need to do myself." He went back to his son, had a strong talk, and has had many more since then. More bad reports came to him about his son in the following weeks. The talks had to get even stronger, and some needed discipline was applied.

In the midst of all this, he took his son on an overnight fishing trip. The only rule? They just had to have a good time! The combination of firmness and a special time away worked wonders for this young man. In a few weeks his whole demeanor had changed; he had become more courteous to others and had begun to make great progress toward becoming a Christian. But without his father's diligence and willingness to change his style, none of this would have happened.

6. Competence

> Do you see a man skilled in his work?
> He will serve before kings;
> he will not serve before obscure men.
> (Proverbs 22:29)

One of the defining elements of true manhood is the possession of skills and the ability of a man to use those skills to support himself and his family. As a father, you need to raise your son to be a skilled and competent man.

Our world seems increasingly populated by young men who are adrift. They are unemployed or under-employed, and they seemingly have little motivation to do anything about it. Many of these young men are college educated but are stuck in low-paying jobs that do not have much future. These young men are the result of the failure of fathers to raise their sons to be productive, energetic members of society.

Help your son to find what he is good at, to work hard at it and to grow in his skills. Some boys are dreamers; they think they have talents that they do not. They dream of becoming a professional athlete or a rock star when that is really not their gift. Help your son to be realistic and to invest his life in something more down-to-earth. Help him to be good at whatever he likes to do, but help him to be wise in assessing his talent level. Only a few go to the upper levels in the fields of sports or music; most others should just enjoy their talents and use them as a way to round out and enrich their lives.

Other boys are unmotivated and lack confidence that they can do anything well. Sometimes they look at others, perhaps an older brother or an older friend, and they feel they come up short. It is vital for you as the father of a young man like this to help him discover his abilities and talents. The longer I live, the more convinced I am that everyone is gifted, they just need to discover what their gifts are. A wise and loving father can make a huge difference in the life of a young man who needs to discover what he can do well.

As I said earlier, not every young boy is going to make straight As or be a powerful leader or a great athlete. So what? God does not ask us to be something he did not create us to be; he does ask us to be the best version of ourselves that we can be. Do not fall into the trap of pushing your son beyond his talents just to satisfy your, or his, pride.

My sons, David and Jonathan, are very different from one another. David is almost naturally disciplined and organized, and he finds it rather easy to step forward and lead others. Jonathan, like David, is an excellent student, but he has to work harder at being organized. Jonathan is a excellent leader, but he leads in a different way than his brother. David is able to get the whole group organized and inspired; Jonathan senses what is in the heart and soul of a group and uses that to motivate them. I have had to realize their differences and to develop both boys in their areas of natural ability. I have also had to help them to overcome their areas of weakness. And I have tried to do all of this without undermining their confidence. I am sure that you, like me, will often find yourself asking God (and others around you) for wisdom in this most challenging of responsibilities. So, my goal has been to help them develop their strengths and work through their weaknesses to the point that both of them can live successful lives.

7. Discipline, Hard Work and Responsibility

> The way of the sluggard is blocked with
> thorns,
>   but the path of the upright is a highway.
> (Proverbs 15:19)

Teach your son the value of hard work, discipline and responsibility. Teach him the value of being prompt in all of his appointments and of being true to his word. If he says he is going to do something, then he needs to do it. Once he is given something to do, he should be trusted to do it without fail.

Many of us have allowed our sons to be lazy while Mom and Dad do all the work around the house. If you are doing this, you are not helping him. You instead are teaching him that others exist to serve and take care of him, and he has no responsibility. This is a grave mistake, one that will hurt your son for the rest of his life. Early on, give your son jobs to do. Do not overload him when he is little, but give him enough to do to teach him to be responsible. Teach your son to help his mother with some of the household chores. Get him to help you with some of your jobs around the house. If you do this, he will mature rapidly and will develop a sense of righteousness and responsibility—and he will much more likely be converted to God and his kingdom.

Some parents encourage their children to work in jobs outside the home that demand a great deal of time and effort. While it is fine for a young person to learn to work and to have a job and make his own money, I believe some parents go too far with this. Their kids work so many hours a week that it limits their time with their families and teen ministries. Do not allow yourself to be consumed with worry about paying for college. Your child's spiritual growth and relationship with the family is far more important than that. Put first things first, save all you can, and God will provide what you need!

~

I have tried in this chapter to convict you of possible neglect, to inspire you to see how important you are to your son, and to give you practical guidance in raising him. I hope you now have a greater sense of the immense importance of your role. It is unique. There is no one in your son's life like you. Perhaps it may seem that your son does not need you, that he is busy with his own life and with his friends. Perhaps you even feel that other men are more important to him than you. How wrong you are, and you need to realize this before it is too late. There is no one in your son's life like his father!

God has created an almost mystical bond between fathers and sons. Some of us may have never developed that bond with our sons, but the potential is there, and the opportunity is still there. Do not retreat from your son in discouragement, fear, frustration or apathy. Reach out to him. Go after him. Love him. Let him know how special he is to you and how you want to be the father that he needs. Pour yourself out. Don't hold back; you have nothing to lose but your pride. You have everything to gain. You can still build a relationship with your son that will save his soul, bring you indescribable joy, and give you a peace that you will carry into your old age.

NOTES

1. Sam Laing, *Mighty Man of God*, (Billerica, Mass.: Discipleship Publications International, 1999).

Father and Daughter

6

Elizabeth

My hero will forever be a man who is 5'8", slightly bowlegged, and would wear orange clothing every day of his life if he could get away with it...a man who longs to be not only a preacher, but also a novelist, a football coach, a multilingual scholar/historian, a farmer, a librarian and a grocery store manager...all while living in the country and riding a Harley-Davidson...with a cat on his shoulder.

My dad is among the most fascinating and wonderful, multifaceted men God ever made...and I absolutely adore him. My favorite memories with him are too numerous to even attempt to describe. The earliest are of times in elementary school when Dad would come home from work and ask me to go running with him. Immediately my heart would skip a beat, and I would breathe "Yes" as I dashed upstairs to put on my sneakers. We would run together until my little legs turned to rubber, but I would have run forever just to be with him.

I remember those nights in high school and college when Dad would look at me with a gleam in his eye and ask, "You wanna go see a movie?" Again I would sprint pell-mell up the stairs to grab my purse, and we'd fly out the door, five minutes late every time.

And then there is my wedding day. Only a few minutes remained before we were to walk down the aisle, and all the bridesmaids had already lined up, leaving the two of us alone. We prayed together, both of us fighting back tears. When we finished, I got so nervous and excited that I suddenly became terribly hot and flushed. Dad found an enormous piece of cardboard lying on the floor, and as I held my arms straight out to the side, he stood ten feet away from me and awkwardly fanned me with the cardboard, our laughter mingling with our tears.

A girl's relationship with her dad molds so much of who she is. Most importantly, it teaches her how to be a child of God and how to understand God's love. It teaches her what it means to love and be close to a man, and it prepares her for her marriage one day.

A father's relationship with his daughter is very different from a mother's, especially as girls enter their preteen and early teen years. It may seem harder for fathers to be as close to their daughters; suddenly there are all kind of womanly changes going on that a father can't relate to or even discuss.

I remember when, at twelve, my mom finally let me start shaving my legs. This was a major event in my preteen life—in my mind a huge step toward womanhood. I wasn't about to talk about this with Dad, but apparently Mom told him about it. Later that evening he came into my room and simply rubbed his hand on my now smooth ankle and smiled at me, thus letting me know that he was aware of my new step toward womanhood. It was the first of a number of changes in my life that Dad would know about, but not participate directly in.

My relationship with him remained of paramount importance, and I needed him more than I ever had before—just in different ways. Girls desperately need their fathers to have certain characteristics to help them make it through their teenage years. These are the same characteristics that will keep them deeply bonded even through the years of change.

1. Strength

> Moreover, we have all had human fathers who disciplined us and we respected them for it. How much more should we submit to the Father of our spirits and live! Our fathers disciplined us for a little while as they thought best. (Hebrews 12:9-10a)

A girls needs to see that her father is strong. He should be the major disciplinarian and authority figure in his daughter's life, possessing solid, uncompromising convictions and standards for himself and for his children. A father's strength takes pressure off his wife, allowing her to focus on her roles of nurturing, comforting, listening and encouraging.

As I became a teenager, Mom and I talked all the time, but the same was not true in my relationship with Dad. Certainly we still talked a great deal and he always knew what was going on in my life, but the day-in, day-out, detailed discussions were handled more by Mom. Dad usually stepped in for significant discipling events and issues, for persistent struggles I faced, or when I came to him for help. And when Dad got involved, things changed. An important conversation with Dad was always memorable. It's not that my dad was harsh, overly intense or constantly rebuking or threatening; rather, his words, however gentle, carried a weight to them that no one else's did.

When I was about sixteen, I went through a period when I began to criticize my mom. I started noticing her flaws and holding them against her, no longer respecting her as I should have. This went on for a while, with little change on my part. I vividly remember the day Dad stepped in and we talked, sitting together on my bed. I will never forget his tears as he told me how much he adored Mom and how much it hurt him to see me treat her that way. My heart broke, and I wept. I could not stand hurting my dad, and his tears helped me realize how unfair and cruel I was being toward my mom. I changed from that moment on.

Dad did not rebuke me on that particular occasion, but there were certainly times when he did. And in those times he would not back down until I repented, not just in action but in heart. Dad never settled for simple acquiescence or partial obedience, but only for true repentance. His righteous anger was a thing that inspired respect and a healthy fear in all the kids. We knew that there was to be absolutely no crossing Dad in our family.

An aspect of his strength that particularly helped me during my teenage years was his logic and reasoning. I was so often propelled entirely by my emotions, but talking to Dad helped me sift through my feelings in a rational and calm manner. He sympathized with my emotions, but also knew how to separate feeling from fact. Dad could always give me a plan of action when I needed to change something difficult—a simple plan that I could follow, even at my most irrational moments.

Dad has had to be particularly strong with Alexandra. She has sometimes taken him on and argued with him, and he has had to win a battle of wills with her. He has refused to tolerate any disrespect from her, however subtle. His strength and consistency in dealing with this are helping Alexandra learn true humility and submission to God, and will prepare her to one day be a humble wife as well.

2. Spirituality

> Love the LORD your God with all your heart and with all your soul and with all your strength. These commandments that I give you today are to be upon your hearts. Impress them on your children. Talk about them when you sit at home and when you walk along the road, when you lie down and when you get up. (Deuteronomy 6:5-7)

The thing that inspired us to respect our dad more than anything else was his relationship with God. I have never known anyone to walk with God as he does. His relationship with God is his passion and his driving force. Morning after morning, I saw him disappear into the woods behind our house to pray and meditate, often for hours at a time. Our family prayed together regularly, and he consistently shared the Bible with us.

This spirituality allowed me to trust my dad implicitly. I never doubted anything he said because I knew that above all he was a man of God. And I was inspired to strive for a relationship with God that would somehow mirror my father's. His love for God made me love God and him even more than I already did.

3. Vulnerability

> We have spoken freely to you...and opened wide our hearts to you. We are not withholding our affection from you, but you are withholding yours from us. As a fair exchange...open wide your hearts also.
> (2 Corinthians 6:11-13)

My Dad was always strong, but there was so much more to him than just strength. He was not afraid to show his true emotions. His strength inspired my respect and obedience; his spirituality earned my admiration, but his vulnerability won my heart.

Most women can count on one hand the times they have seen their fathers cry, if ever. I cannot even remember all the times I have seen my dad tear up. He has never been too afraid or proud to show his true feelings, and I love his soft heart. I have seen him cry just talking about God, describing his love for Mom or one of us or during moments of grief. I still remember the day he told me about his regrets in his relationship with his own father, and the tears we shed together as he spoke.

Dad has always gone out of his way to express his love and affection for us. He envelops us in the most wonderful bear hugs, and gives great shoulder massages. He disciplines us, but he is equally generous with his praise. That expressiveness did more for my confidence as a young woman than anything else could have. I respected Dad with all my heart and felt that if he loved me, then I must not be that bad after all. If everything was great between Dad and me, then all was right with the world.

Preteen girls and young teens are tremendously insecure, but if they have the affection of an adoring father, they will be far more confident. In addition, they will be far less likely to seek confidence and affection from young men if those needs are being met by their fathers. If they see a healthy and vibrant love between their parents, they will want to wait for such a love themselves. I often prayed that God would give me a man who looked at me the way I saw Dad looking at Mom.

Vulnerability also means carrying yourself with humility and being honest with your family about your own weaknesses and sins. It means apologizing when you hurt their feelings or lose your temper. Dad never made us feel that he was on some higher plane of righteousness than the rest of the world; he frequently shared with us his own struggles and sinful nature. One of the things that helped me most as I wrestled with arrogance and selfish ambition was hearing Dad describe his struggles as a young disciple with those same sins.

4. Involvement

> For you know that we dealt with each of
> you as a father deals with his own children,
> encouraging, comforting and urging you to
> live lives worthy of God, who calls you into
> his kingdom and glory. (1 Thessalonians 2:
> 11-12)

Fathers may not provide as much intensive input into their daughters' daily lives as mothers do, but there are so many other ways to remain involved. You may be tempted to feel a bit distanced from your daughter as she matures, but do not allow this to happen. Look for ways to be involved in her life.

Dad was always my biggest fan in everything I did. His faith in me inspired me to dream and to do greater things than I would have done on my own. He supported, encouraged and edited my writing wholeheartedly. When I ran for student government positions, he helped me write my speeches. In the seventh grade, I was a miler on the track team, and with practice only twice a week, I didn't feel ready for our first big meet. I came home from school the day before the meet crying because I felt unprepared. That night Dad took me running to help me "train"—in reality that run probably just wore me out the night before the race, but it did worlds of good for my confidence and peace of mind. He even gave me instructions on what to eat and when to eat it to yield maximum energy the next day. When I ran again in high school, he helped me come up with summer training regimens and goals. All those things kept us feeling connected throughout my teenage years.

Dads, you can stay close to your daughters; it just takes extra thoughtfulness, sensitivity and sacrifice on your part. Consistently look for ways to involve yourself in your daughter's interests.

5. Fun

> ...a time to laugh... (Ecclesiastes 3:4)

Young teens are all about one thing: fun. They love to laugh deliriously and act like absolute goons—and their ideas of what is hilarious and fun generally seem profoundly stupid to everyone else but themselves. Their silliness can tend to inspire the opposite reaction in everyone around them. That is, others become tense, rigid and annoyed, and long for peace and quiet. Fathers, if you want to remain close to your daughters, loosen up and have fun with them. Remember the silly games you played when they were three, and how stupid you felt? Be prepared to revive those days, thirteen-year-old style, and to throw out all your stuffiness and dignity. I guarantee, if you can make your daughter laugh—even better, if you can make her friends laugh (without coming across as dorky!)—then you will have her heart forever. And if you can't do that, at least allow yourself to enjoy her laughter with her friends.

∿

> When I was a [girl] in my father's house,
> still tender and an only child of
> my mother,

he taught me and said,
  "Lay hold of my words with all
      your heart;
keep my commands and you will live."
(Proverbs 4:3-4)

Fathers, you only get to be the man in your daughter's life for a few short years; do not squander them. Cherish your daughter, adore her, discipline her, and make time for her now, before it is too late and another man takes your place. Tell her she's beautiful, hug her every chance you get, and teach her everything you know about God and about life. Girls want to feel their fathers' love more than anything in the world...and if you offer it, she will surely hand you her heart with unquestioning loyalty and trust. And even though one day you walk her down the aisle and give her away to another man, you'll both secretly know that she will forever remain her daddy's girl.

7

Mother and Son

Geri

> Then [Jesus] went down to Nazareth with
> them and was obedient to them. But his
> mother treasured all these things in her
> heart. And Jesus grew in wisdom and
> stature, and in favor with God and men.
>
> Luke 2:51-52

Mary's panic and imagination must have run
wild. She and Joseph had been traveling for a day,
assuming that Jesus was somewhere among their
company, only to discover that he was nowhere to
be seen. Three long days later they found him listening to and speaking with the Jewish teachers at
the temple back in Jerusalem. As a mother, she had
probably pictured her son in countless scenarios,
all of them devastating! When they found him
healthy, happy and safe, she and Joseph were
relieved and yet understandably angry. "Son, why
have you treated us like this?" was Mary's response.
Jesus said that it was time to be about his Father's
business. As a twelve-year-old son it signified

Jesus' first steps away from his parents, out of childhood and into adulthood; but his parents "did not understand..." (Luke 2:50).

I don't know if there is anything quite so amazing and yet unnerving for a mother than to watch the transformation of her little boy into young adulthood. Almost overnight everything changes, from his shoe size to the sound of his voice! With the physical changes come so many emotional and social changes. No longer does he allow himself to be hugged and kissed—at least not publicly. He vacillates between insecurity and loud arrogance. And he becomes aware of girls, sometimes liking them, other times terrified of them. As mothers we may not know who and what we need to be in our sons' lives anymore. Some of us pull away from our sons; others of us hover like overprotective hens.

Mothers, your job is far from over. Your sons need you now more than ever before. Just as Mary had to adjust and grow in her relationship with her preteen son, so we, too, must grow and change along with our maturing sons. We must find that delicate balance between "letting go" and "holding on." As the most important woman in their young lives, we will serve as an example to them of a godly woman. The influence and guidance that we continue to give is profoundly important and will affect everything from their confidence in themselves to the kind of future husbands or leaders they will be.

There are several things we can and must be to help our sons make that difficult transition from boy to man.

1. Tender

Remember when your boy was small and came to you crying because of a skinned knee or some other injury or hurt? You probably put him on your lap, held him and miraculously kissed the hurt away. After a few minutes he usually ran off happy with everything "all better." If only we could fix everything so quickly and easily as our children get older! As they grow up, the hurts are more often wounded feelings and bruised egos rather than scraped knees and elbows, yet they still need to be loved and comforted.

It is amazing how unaffectionate we can become as our sons move away from the childhood years. Some of the warmest, most compassionate mothers become no-nonsense and almost businesslike as their children get older.

Adolescents and teens still need affection and warmth! They need to be hugged and touched and yes, even appropriately kissed. Of course, it changes, but affection must not disappear. Even our sons need warm smiles of love and approval. We often have no idea how very much our sons need our physical expressions of love and tenderness. I remember Jonathan once telling me that when he got lonely at school, he would just think of me smiling and he would feel happier. You can be sure that made me want to smile a lot more.

2. Constant

> [Love] always protects, always trusts, always hopes, always perseveres.
> (1 Corinthians 13:7)

The adolescent years are filled with insecurities and confusion. Your son may be convinced that he is the biggest "nerd" in the world—especially in his school and among his peers. The whole world, or so it seems to him, thinks he is a misfit because of his standards and morals. He needs to know that you believe with all of your being that he is special and wonderful.

Tell him specifically what you like about him, what his unique gifts and abilities are. I believe God made every person with special talents and strengths. But many of us go through our entire lives never really thinking we are good at anything. We have talents and abilities that lie undiscovered and undeveloped. Some of these are physical abilities such as intelligence, athletic prowess or musical talent. But I am talking about even more important strengths and gifts—strengths of character such as integrity, kindness and the ability to encourage people or make people laugh. Tell your son what you love and like about him. See in him the good things he cannot see in himself. Tell him how much you love him. Say it over and over again!

Encourage your son when he succeeds. Be his greatest fan and most loyal supporter. Encourage him when he fails. He needs to know you still believe in him, love him and like him. Our son Jonathan ran cross-country throughout his teen years. The last race of the season was the one in which he hoped to qualify to run in the state meet. He ran an incredible race and was coming in at the end of the race in seventh place on the team—the last possible spot that would allow him to run in the state meet. We all thought he had done it, and we were cheering for him. With twenty yards to go one of his teammates came from behind and passed him. By the time Jonathan saw him, he had nothing left and, in the end, lost his place. He was so disappointed and was berating himself that he had not given his best.

A few days later someone gave us a picture of Jonathan and his teammate as they were coming in "neck and neck." Jonathan's face in the picture told the whole story—he was pushing as hard as he was physically able to push. I put that picture up on the refrigerator for Jonathan to look at. I wanted to encourage him and remind him that he had given all he had to give. He had run the best race he was able to run, and he could be proud. I still believed in him and was proud of him and especially proud of what he had given to the team. The picture is still there to remind him of that.

Raising preteens and teens is a difficult task, requiring incredible patience and wisdom. There will be many times when our sons fail miserably. Sometimes they will need to be encouraged and lifted back up. At other times they will need firm discipline, a hard talk, punishment and consequences. But through it all, there is never a time to stop loving, caring or believing in our children. They may feel very keenly our disappointment in them, but they must also know that we have not given up on them or stopped loving them.

3. Practical

So much of our job as mothers is teaching our children "how to be." It concerns me greatly as I see so many children who are not being taught the basic social graces. We are not teaching our children, and I would say especially our young men, the fundamentals of politeness and grace. Then we complain about the rudeness of today's teenagers! We must teach our sons to be polite and well mannered. They need practical instruction on how to speak respectfully and intelligibly to adults, to open doors for women, to clean up after themselves at home and at someone else's home, to have good table manners...and the list goes on and on.

Proverbs 31:21-31 is a beautiful description of a mother who is involved in the day-to-day life of her family as she "watches over the affairs of her household." She helps them with the practical things of life such as food and clothing. Our children need to be fed healthy, nutritious meals. Boys love to come home to the aroma of real food and a set table—not just bags of fast food scattered across the kitchen counter. Their memories will be of Mom's cooking and meals around the table long after they are grown and gone.

Many young men would welcome a mother's touch to their appearances. Most young men feel so ugly in their adolescent years—too small, too big, too fat, big ears, crooked teeth. Moms, do whatever you can to help your boys look sharp and up-to-date. Without becoming worldly or overly obsessed with appearance, help them with their clothes, haircuts, etc. They will be forever grateful that you understood and that you were watching out for them.

4. Communicative

Perhaps one of the greatest gifts a mother can give her son is the gift of openness and communication.

Mothers, talk to your sons and listen carefully to the things that they say. Boys need to be able to (and must learn to) express the things on their minds and hearts. They need to express their worries and fears as well as the things they are interested in and excited about. Be genuinely interested and be willing to stop and listen when they need to talk. Learn to ask questions without making them feel interrogated and give advice without sounding like a "nag." (See chapter 11 for specifics about how to draw out what your child is thinking.)

I cherish the countless talks I have had with my boys over the years. Many of our talks occurred spontaneously, as we rode in the car together or when I went into their rooms to say good night or as I was preparing a meal. Some talks were of great meaning and profundity while others were the casual sharing of their lives—reliving the victories and defeats of their days. These are the talks that have made us close and will keep us close forever.

∿

As mothers, we have a very special place and a unique role in the raising of our sons. As they learn to talk and be close to us, we are preparing them one day to talk and be close to their wives. I have counseled many women over the years who yearned for a husband who would talk to them. What a blessing that you can influence your son during these early stages and help him to be a sensitive and loving husband someday.

As special and important as a mother's relationship is to her son, you must be very careful never to undermine your son's relationship with his dad. Sometimes it may be easier to talk to Mom. We may seem softer and less intimidating, or perhaps we see needs more quickly. This is understandable, but it must never lead to a situation where Mom and son are close and talk freely while Dad is kept at a distance. Encourage your son to talk to his father. You can become a bridge in your son's relationship with his father. You may perhaps be the first to sense a need in your son's life, and then you and your husband can work together to help him.

Don't ever underestimate the importance of a mother's love in a young man's life. You are irreplaceable—an unending source of love that will comfort him and support him in a world that is big and too often without love. Long after he is grown, the love and guidance you gave him will still be felt. Only then will it be fully appreciated and like the mother of Proverbs 31, you will hear your son arise and call you blessed.

Mother and Daughter

8

Elizabeth

> I do not concern myself with great matters
>   or things too wonderful for me.
> But I have stilled and quieted my soul;
>   like a weaned child with its mother,
>   like a weaned child is my soul
>   within me.
>
> Psalm 131:1b-2

"Pretty is as pretty does." "It's not the feathers on the chicken, it's the stuffing." "All you can do is all you can do." "You know and I know that...(insert some profound truth here)." These are just a few of my mother's most memorable lines. Actually, the first two come from her mother, and I know that I will pass these sayings on to my children...along with a few of my own. There is nothing quite like a mother's wisdom.

Safety, friendship, laughter, compassion, wisdom, understanding, teaching...these are the words that spring to mind when I think of my mom. A mother's role in the life of a preteen and young teen girl is immeasurably important. As I entered my preteen years, I relied upon my mom as never before. I needed to talk...a lot. I needed to be understood and reassured...every day. And I needed answers...about everything.

Indeed Mom must have felt as if all she did some days was listen to me and talk to me. I think I nearly wore her out at times, but she was somehow always available, never too busy, tired or preoccupied.

When girls hit their preteen years, they begin to think a great deal about life, about God, about their relationships, about popularity. They experience insecurity as never before and often face challenges in building friendships. The opposite gender may suddenly become the most fascinating life-form they have ever observed. They are becoming aware of who they are and what they want out of life. Some begin to question everything they ever believed and wonder whether or not their parents' choices are the ones they want for themselves. And perhaps most frightening of all, they feel themselves becoming sinners.

I vividly recall the growing realization that I was no longer a little girl as I experienced the first pains of wrestling with my sinful nature. It felt to me as if a heavy blackness were descending upon my once carefree heart as I faced my own pride, conceit and selfishness. I remember as a sixth grader sitting on my bed and thinking that I didn't think I had what it took to become a disciple; it seemed so easy for my parents but it was just too hard for me.

Feelings like this are very real and need to be talked about. The most important thing a mother can do for her daughter is to be there to listen, talk and advise. Make yourself available as much as possible. These countless conversations will ultimately pave the way for your daughter to become a disciple. They may seem insignificant, tedious or repetitive, but believe me—they are worth the trouble. In the end they will make an enormous difference in your daughter's emotional and spiritual growth and well-being.

I do not remember the subjects of many of my conversations with my mother during those years, but I do recall the peace, wisdom and confidence I walked away with every time. And all those small conversations over the years ultimately served as stepping-stones to larger growth in my life. They planted small seeds of faith, love for God and his mission, peace and confidence—seeds that eventually blossomed into my baptism as a teenager and my faithfulness to Christ.

If a mother fosters an open relationship with her children from their earliest childhood, then as they mature they will probably continue being open with her. My mom was close to each child in our family throughout our developmental years, and so as we reached our preteen years, we did not want to shut her out and retreat into our own selfish, closed worlds. But some preteens and teens will not be so readily open. Perhaps they naturally tend to be somewhat reticent; maybe they haven't had a close relationship with you growing up; perhaps they have simply become more inward as they have grown older. It is a mother's job to attempt to draw out her children and to become close to them even if they are not readily open:

> The purposes of a [girl's] heart are
> deep waters,
> but a [mother] of understanding draws
> them out. (Proverbs 20:5)

However, be careful not to push too hard. There are ways of drawing out your daughter without nagging, pressuring or constantly questioning her. Forcing children to be open often serves to alienate them further as they retreat in pride, rebellion and fear. Unfortunately there is no easy formula to follow in this arena; and only prayer, discipling from other parents, and experimentation with different approaches will yield the method that works best for your daughter.

Mom Doesn't Know Best

While openness and talking are essential for a girl's growth, there is often a huge obstacle that stands in the way of it: the "Mom Doesn't Know Best Syndrome." A strange phenomenon tends to occur in the heart of a young girl as she enters puberty: suddenly she discovers that she has been endowed with a wisdom far superior to that of her mother. She also possesses an uncanny ability to detect every flaw her mother possesses.

Symptoms of this syndrome include criticalness, haughtiness, rebellion and confidence that she knows best about everything, from what she should wear to what route her mom should take driving her to school. She begins dismissing her mother's every suggestion in favor of her own ideas because they are obviously so much better.

My Daughter Is Still a Little Girl

This phenomenon in pubescent girls is somewhat contagious; however, when it spreads to their mothers it mutates into the infamous "My Daughter Is Still a Little Girl Syndrome." Mothers have a difficult time adjusting to the fact that their daughters are indeed maturing and that they should no longer be treated as young girls. If you ever "catch" this syndrome, you will find that symptoms include the following: refusal to allow your daughter any increased freedom, an insistence on still picking out every item of clothing for her (including matching hair bows and socks), making her feel stupid when she tries to behave more like a grown-up, and constantly correcting and nagging her.

As girls become young women, a marked change in their relationship with their mothers occurs. When you combine the two syndromes, it makes for some clashing emotions. The daughter is beginning to mature and wants to be treated as such. As she grows in insight, she may begin realizing that her mother has flaws just like everyone else. She may become critical, arrogant and disrespectful. The mother, perhaps resentful because of her daughter's sin and new desire for independence, resists acknowledging that her child is indeed becoming a young woman. She may still attempt to treat her and discipline her in the exact same way she did when she was a young girl—and such methods only make things worse.

My sister hit this stage a bit earlier than I did, when she first entered puberty at around ten years of age. She thought she knew better than my mom and would take her on, arguing and attempting to manipulate her. I hit this point when I was a bit older, around age sixteen. I suddenly realized that my mother had flaws. I held those things against her and became critical and competitive with her. In my blind conceit I thought I was smarter and at times more spiritual than my mom. First of all, Alexandra and I both needed to have our behinds kicked (figuratively, of course!) for our arrogance and know-it-all attitudes. I still remember the tears I shed as I finally understood the extent of my folly, arrogance and ingratitude.

Forging Ahead

Once we repented of our pride and criticalness, we had to learn how to bond with Mom as maturing young women who were no longer little girls. At times it seemed to each of us as if we were forging an entirely new relationship with her. She began to treat us as young women (albeit very emotional young women!), talking to us and discipling us in a more mature way than ever before.

Moms, be prepared for this difficult transition. Your daughter may buck you, criticize you, or try to shut you out for a while—but do not lose heart! Do not take her sin personally or let it shake your confidence as a mother. Rather, remain confident and calm as you disciple, teach and rebuke your daughter. In some cases, it may take the intervention of your husband or another disciple to show your daughter the extent of her sin and arrogance and to help her become truly thankful for you. When she finally does repent, be completely gracious and forgive unconditionally so that your relationship does not suffer further distance or damage. Again, with prayer, wise counsel and patience, you can survive this transition successfully. Put your hope in the fact that once you make the adjustments in your relationship, you will be far closer than you ever were before. In fact, you will be well on your way to truly becoming best friends as your daughter matures.

WHAT SHE NEEDS

The key roles you play in your daughter's life involve listening and talking; however, she does not need you to simply be her sounding board. She needs you to teach, train and disciple her. There are several key areas in which a daughter needs her mother's teaching.

Help Her Think Spiritually

> My [daughter], keep your father's
>   commands
>   and do not forsake your mother's
>   teaching.
> Bind them upon your heart forever;
>   fasten them around your neck.
> When you walk, they will guide you;
>   when you sleep, they will watch
>   over you;
>   when you awake, they will speak
>   to you.
> For these commands are a lamp,
>   this teaching is a light,
> and the corrections of discipline
>   are the way to life. (Proverbs 6:20-23)

Even when your daughter is baptized, she will not automatically think in a spiritual manner. Your discipling job is far from over! Like any young Christian, her first response to situations may be worldly, faithless or prideful. But talking through things with you should provide her with the guidance to learn to think as God would want her to. Don't be afraid to open the Bible with her! In fact, she needs to learn to apply the Bible to her daily life. For example, if she comes to you describing difficult situations with friends at school, you can use the opportunity to teach her how God wants us to handle conflict by applying such passages as Matthew 18:15-16.

Some situations may not require a lengthy speech detailing how she should handle her life. Often you may only need to ask the right questions to help her start thinking spiritually on her own. You may ask questions such as "What's the right thing to do?" "What's the righteous way to handle that?" "What could you have said differently?" "How would Jesus look at that?" "What does the Bible say?" and so on. But the key is not simply to give advice, but to give godly counsel, teaching her to think for herself in the process.

Help Her Feel Normal

There must be some hormone that courses through our bodies at puberty convincing us that we are different and weird. Girls begin to believe that they are all alone in their feelings, thoughts and temptations, and this can cause them to pull back not only from you but from the rest of the world as well. These feelings can paralyze them with insecurity.

As a preteen and teenager, I was convinced that I was different from everyone else around me. I felt everything acutely and was painfully insecure. Even after becoming a Christian, I was convinced that my sins were far worse than others' sins. I often felt overwhelmed by guilt, but terrified to discuss my horrible sins with other disciples. My mom had to tell me over and over again that I was normal, that my temptations were no different from anyone else's and that I could therefore be open with others. Even when I had a difficult time believing her, she never gave up repeating the same truths as many times as I needed to hear them.

Help Her Be Confident

Insecurity is the bane of adolescence. I still remember agonizing moments of embarrassment that made me feel as if the entire world were laughing at me. I have never forgotten the line Mom repeated so many times: "Nobody's looking at you or laughing at you. They're too busy worrying what you're thinking about them." I also remember her teaching me how to be confident and friendly toward people at school. She shared with me the story of how, in high school, she had overcome her own insecurity and quietness by walking the school hallways deliberately making eye-contact, smiling brightly and saying "Hi" to anyone she passed.

Tell your daughter she's beautiful, and help her see her strengths, even when she feels she has none. Praise her for the things she is good at; believe it or not, she values your opinion and encouragement more than almost anyone else's.

Help her dress cool, and when she is old enough, you might consider teaching her how to apply a little makeup. If you don't know what's cool, help her find out. Some of her insecurities might be somewhat justified if her clothes and hair are completely outdated, and if she has no idea how to look cool. I am not talking about becoming worldly or obsessed with the exterior, but appearance is important to young women (and to young men!). If your daughter does not feel confident in her appearance, she really will suffer in ways you can help her avoid.

I have worked with young women in various campus ministries on this issue. Coming into college, they knew little about how to dress or otherwise enhance their physical appearance, and as a result they lacked a great deal of confidence. Many of them were known in high school as being shy, quiet and awkward in social settings. It has been amazing to see them blossom as their friends in the campus ministry have helped them learn how to shop, dress and wear their hair and makeup. Not only have they become more beautiful, but their entire demeanor has transformed as well. They have grown markedly more confident and outgoing. And perhaps most exciting of all from the girls' perspective has been the improvement in their dating lives. Whenever I have seen young women make these changes, I have felt happy for them, but I also have wished they had learned these things as teenagers and experienced such confidence earlier in life.

Mothers, help your daughters! If you are clueless about what is cool, get help from someone, and provide your daughters with enough money to buy what they need. Believe me, that money will be well spent.

Help Her Get Discipling

> He who spares the rod hates his son,
> but he who loves him is careful to
> discipline him. (Proverbs 13:24)

> The rod of correction imparts wisdom,
> but a child left to himself disgraces
> his mother. (Proverbs 29:15)

My main regret from my teen years is that I was not as open with or close to other disciples as I should have been. Not only did I avoid receiving correction, but I also "avoided" receiving the encouragement my vulnerability could have brought. I was overly concerned with what people thought of me, and deeply afraid of discipling. I allowed my pride, insecurity and fear to control me, and as a result I only felt comfortable talking to my mom about certain things. Had I been more consistently and vulnerably open, I would have learned that my temptations and sins were normal, and that others shared my exact struggles. Instead, I was left feeling, in spite of Mom's continual reassurances, that I was different from other people, and that I could not trust them with my true thoughts and feelings. Even now I am still learning how to trust people enough to be deeply open with them. I am working hard to embrace discipling instead of fearing and avoiding it. I wish I had pushed through these struggles more as a teen. If I had, how much easier my life (and my mother's life) would have been and how much more I could have grown.

One of the worst mistakes some mothers make is shielding their children from others' discipling. It is healthy for them to receive correction and rebuke from others. Some mothers baby and protect their daughters from such input because they worry that they are too fragile or immature to handle it. Instead of supporting and thanking the teen workers for their efforts to disciple and save their children, these mothers resist the help. If your daughter repeatedly responds poorly to discipling, even on small matters, chances are that the problem is not her immaturity, delicate emotions or imperfect discipler, but rather her own pride. Let other people challenge her, and do not undermine their efforts by getting defensive on her behalf or by questioning their judgment. Support them by urging your daughter to be open with them and to listen to their advice, and by following up with talks at home. In the end, you are not only helping your daughter to grow, but you are also doing yourself a big favor. This will take some pressure off your relationship with your daughter by keeping you from always being the "bad guy" pointing out things she needs to change.

Certainly there may be a time to step in if you believe your daughter is really being treated wrongly, but it has been my experience that those times are actually quite rare. A little correction, whether perfectly worded or not, never hurt anybody; so let God teach your child as he sees fit. If you do, she will grow and mature quickly and will one day adjust smoothly when she transitions from the teen ministry to the campus ministry.

Pray with Your Daughter

You can spend countless hours listening to and talking with your daughter, but the ultimate lesson you can impart to her is the importance of prayer. Any time Mom and I had a major discussion about something in my life, she always initiated a prayer together afterward. I wonder if sometimes she did this because she honestly didn't know what else to say to me or how to help me! I remember crying through many shaky prayers after our emotional discussions. Those prayers reminded me that God was my ultimate discipler and the one who could fix my problems—not my mother. Those prayers helped to calm my feelings and to get me thinking spiritually, even when I couldn't seem to conjure a spiritual thought. Prayer works, and prayer can bond you and your daughter as nothing else will.

∿

I treasure my relationship with my mother more than almost anything on earth. I could spend days alone with her and not be bored for even a moment. In that time we would surely discuss every nuance of our feelings and thoughts, map out the rest of our dream lives in detail, choose spouses for every single person we know, and solve the world's problems...after ardently expressing our opinions about all of them, of course. Most of what I know about life has come from my mother. I consciously and unconsciously imitate and quote her every day. I can anticipate her word-for-word response in almost any situation.

Now that I am married and have my own home, there are so many things I do just because my mother did them—from keeping books next to the toilet to making little piles of papers everywhere to freezing grease in empty soup cans. She is my mentor, hero, friend and one of the greatest blessings of my life. It may be difficult to imagine such a relationship while in the midst of the trying teenage years, but do not lose hope! In time, with the help of God and his people, you and your daughter can move through these years victoriously, building a friendship to treasure for a lifetime.

Sibling Relationships

9

Elizabeth

How good and pleasant it is
when [siblings] live together in unity!
It is like precious oil poured on the head,
running down on the beard.
Psalm 133:1-2

Tears streamed down her face as she shared her memories about her brother, the groom, at the wedding rehearsal dinner. She said that their relationship had been so perfect that she could not recall even one argument between them in their entire lives. Listening to her recollections, I felt somewhat surprised and disbelieving. I was happy for them (and their parents!) because they had such a unique relationship, but I thought to myself that they were truly a rarity.

For the vast majority of people, sibling relationships are far from easy to maintain, particularly during the turbulent preteen and early teen years. In fact, they are among the most challenging issues faced by many preteens and young teens as they mature, and especially as they become disciples. God uses these relationships as a crucible in which our young characters are exposed and refined. Our interactions with our siblings have a way of revealing our true character and sinful nature as nothing else does. They provide innumerable and invaluable discipling opportunities. Oftentimes the sins most exposed by sibling relationships are the very sins young teens must repent of in order to become disciples. Therefore, if discipling and repentance occur, sibling relationships can ultimately become one of the most valuable tools for shaping our lives to be more like Jesus.

Most of my favorite memories of my preteen and early teen years are the times spent with my brothers and sister. I remember my tomboy days playing war games in the woods with my brothers, elaborate fort-building and fiercely competitive ping-pong playing, winter snowball pummeling in the yard and summertime cannonballing in the lake.

In those days the children in our family simply had fun together. As we have grown older, we have become the closest of friends, each of us having a unique relationship with each of the others. But such intimacy was not automatic. And while my memories of our preteen and early teen years are fond ones, there were also moments of sin, discord and discipling. We have worked through many difficulties in order to become close; I know we will continue to do so.

Some parents seem to think that sibling closeness is a magical thing that comes purely from having a group of children who somehow have great "chemistry" together as siblings. They see families whose children are close, and they wish that they, too, had been blessed with "easy" kids who just happened to automatically love each other. I don't care how great your kids are, sibling relationships will expose every weakness and sin they possess. The key to children in a family bonding with one another is not magic, chemistry or luck, but rather the discipling efforts of the parents.

Key to Discipling

> Whoever loves his brother lives in the light, and there is nothing in him to make him stumble. But whoever hates his brother is in the darkness and walks around in the darkness....(1 John 2:10-11a)

Even in the earliest pages of the Bible we see that sibling relationships can bring out the very worst in us. We read in Genesis 4 of two brothers: Abel's righteousness exposed all the worst parts of Cain's character...his jealousy, resentment, anger and self-pity. Sibling rivalry gave birth to the first recorded murder.

Already a challenge, sibling relationships can become a nightmare when the emotional vacillations of puberty enter into the already unstable equation. The temptation during these years may be for parents to throw up their hands in frustration and decide to simply ride out the storm, hoping that one day their children will suddenly outgrow these conflicts. But it has been my experience that pre-teens whose relationships and character go undiscipled during these years only grow worse as they become teenagers, and that sibling relationships not salvaged during these years can be utterly destroyed by the time teens hit high school.

My parents always used our sibling relationships as one of their primary tools for discipling our characters. Each of us had different sins that were exposed by each other. My sins were self-righteousness, defensiveness and arrogance. I also had a selfishness that caused me to withdraw into my own isolated world. My brother David's major sin was being too selfish to deeply love or connect with the rest of us, especially with Jonathan. Jonathan's weaknesses were a hot temper, resentment, deliberately inciting anger in the rest of us and trying to boss Alexandra around. As Alexandra has become a teenager, she has had to deal with her stubbornness and pride (especially in her relationship with Jonathan), with bossiness, and with being pushy and selfish about getting her own way. (By the way, they all gave their permission for me to share these things.)

Interestingly, these exact sins are the very ones that compose our core sinful natures. My parents took advantage of the discipling opportunities provided by the sins we exposed in each other, discipling not just words and actions but heart and character. Had they simply glossed over our disagreements with easy or temporary solutions, not taking the time to teach us the truth about our characters, it would have been much more difficult for us to become disciples later on.

Of all the relationships in our family, Jonathan and Alexandra have had the most difficulty getting along with one another. Their relationship provides a great example of this kind of character discipling.

Jonathan and Alexandra, although they love each other, have a real knack for bringing out the worst in each other. Their pattern has been thus: Jonathan would either attempt to help, correct or disciple Alexandra in some way (sometimes righteously, sometimes unrighteously), and Alexandra would often respond pridefully and defensively without really listening to him. Then, when Alexandra got upset with him, Jonathan would either become angry and militant, attempting to force her to obey him, or else he would poke fun at her and tease her in the way that only older brothers can, first frustrating and then infuriating her. She would then retaliate in anger...you get the picture.

I deeply admire my parents' dogged persistence in dealing with this challenge. It is difficult to sift through the disagreements to figure out who is wrong and who needs discipling, but my parents have not given up. They have kept at it, discipling, correcting, teaching, encouraging and rebuking over and over again. That is not to say that every time Jonathan and Alexandra had a disagreement, Mom and Dad would sit and analyze every part of it, but they have not allowed arguments to linger unresolved. And even though it has sometimes been a real challenge for Jonathan and Alexandra to get along, Mom and Dad have not allowed a state of bickering and disunity to go on within the family. They have refused to allow their quarreling to dominate the mood of our home, in the spirit of Proverbs 17:1:

> Better a dry crust with peace and quiet
> than a house full of feasting, with strife.

They realized early on that Jonathan and Alexandra simply exposed each other's sinful natures, and that if they did not change the weaknesses exposed in their relationship with each other, they would face them again in their relationships with other people. Even now, as Alexandra is seeking to become a disciple, one of the key areas she is focusing on is her relationship with her brother.

Similarly, when David became a disciple, making changes in his sibling relationships was a key part of his conversion. Because he had always possessed a great deal of integrity, even to the point of legalism, David had difficulty seeing his sinful nature. He did not readily see or deeply regret his sins of selfishness, lack of love and aloofness. I still vividly remember the night our family sat down to help David see how he, just like everyone else, had a wretched sinful nature that deeply hurt other people. We all shared with him how we had been affected by his sin, and Jonathan in particular told David how he longed to be close to him but felt held at a distance. That talk was a pivotal time for David because it made his sin real to him as nothing else could have, and because it showed him that he could no longer see himself as the nice, good boy he'd always thought he was.

Recently, as Alexandra has been seeking to become a disciple, my parents sat down with her, along with Jonathan, and had the same kind of talk. That discussion helped Alexandra understand how much her selfishness affects the atmosphere in our home, and how much her pride has pushed our family, and especially Jonathan, away from her at times. After the talk, she even called me and sought my input.

A key to the effectiveness of my parents' discipling in these areas was that once they disciplined and corrected us, they expected true remorse and total repentance. They were not satisfied with mumbled apologies or halfhearted change—and this helped us learn what it meant to truly repent. We knew we couldn't fake our parents out because they were very good at "reading" us. If we gave a perfunctory apology, Dad would tell us to look him in the eyes as he asked, "Is that what you really feel?" We knew Mom and Dad wouldn't drop the matter until they felt confident that we were ready to change.

Along with teaching wholehearted repentance, my parents have always fostered an open atmosphere in our family. No one's sins were a secret, and each of us knew not only our own weaknesses, but everyone else's also. Dad always made it a point to use the discipling received by one child as a teaching opportunity for the whole family. Every time one of us had a discipling time with Dad, he always encouraged us to share what we had learned with the rest of the family at the dinner table. It taught us humility and openness, and fostered closeness among all of us.

Closeness and Affection

> Finally, all of you, live in harmony with one another; be sympathetic, love as brothers, be compassionate and humble. (1 Peter 3:8)

I've addressed many of the challenges faced by brothers and sisters in their relationships with one another, but these negative issues should not dominate the family atmosphere. Overall, sibling relationships—and those of the family as a whole—should be characterized by a deep closeness, friendship and affection.

My family is still my favorite group to be with of any group in the world. Every time we are together, we talk so loudly, excitedly and incessantly that we can barely follow the flow of our own conversation. We laugh until we can barely breathe and tears stream down our faces. And we feel completely at ease, knowing that we are among those who know us the best—for good and for bad—and yet love us the most.

My parents worked hard to foster this atmosphere in our family, especially when we reached the preteen and early teen years and our natural tendency was to pull away.

One of the most crucial things my parents did in those years was to keep dinnertime sacred. As we became old enough, we were all busy with after-school sports and clubs, and with preteen and teen ministry events. But we still had dinner together almost every night. It was such a simple thing, but it kept our family connected. Even when I was in middle school, the highlight of my day was eating dinner with my family. I treasured those times as my refuge during some very difficult years. After spending all day at school battling insecurity, loneliness and the temptations of the world, I could always look forward to being with my family in a fun, happy environment where I could at last just be myself.

In addition to dinnertime, it is so important during these years to continue other special times, traditions and events. These bond a family together in an inexplicable but lasting way. Not only did our family look forward to our vacations, but sometimes I think we looked forward to the car trips themselves even more than our actual vacations! Those were times when we could be together, completely uninterrupted by the outside world. It was during my pre-teen years that we began such Laing family traditions as the sacred "Shoe-Removal Ritual" (I'll spare you the details!), the reading of Sherlock Holmes mysteries and Dave Barry's comedic writings.

Perhaps the most meaningful tradition my parents established was that on birthdays we would all share what we loved about the person having the birthday. What a tremendous and dramatic difference this made in our young hearts! It was so good for us, who were naturally self-consumed and ungrateful, to spend time thinking about all the ways we loved one another. Without fail, we would all end up in tears as we described all the things we loved about the person.

We learned to sincerely appreciate one another, to respect each other and to express that appreciation and respect in a meaningful way. And not only did we feel differently about one another, but we acted differently too. We became more humble, kind and respectful toward one another, and we even went out of our way to continue encouraging and thanking each other. I still remember the tears we have shed and the specific things we have shared about one another—all the things I now appreciate most about the different members of my family.

Age Barriers

Partly because of things like these family traditions and partly because of our short five-year age span, my brothers and I have for the most part always been close. When my sister came along, I was already eleven years old, and her belated entrance into the family added a new twist to the sibling dynamics. We all absolutely adored her and toted her around as if she were our own child. But when I hit my early teen years and began to build a life of my own, with many friends and appointments and plans, it became harder for us to remain truly close. A four-year-old and a fifteen-year-old just don't have coinciding schedules.

It was at that time that we established what is still one of my favorite occasions: Sister Days. We would set aside several hours to be together, designating it a Sister Day. During those times Alexandra and I would do something alone together: eating lunch in a park with cartwheel lessons afterward, baking cookies and renting a movie, painting our toenails and making a collage...whatever the two of us decided upon. Those times bonded us and kept us close throughout my busy teen years. Periodically, the boys would each set aside special times to spend with Alexandra as well, times that kept them close as the boys grew older and busier. Creative traditions like these are crucial for all families, but especially for those with a significant age span among the siblings.

Our family has gone through some huge changes in the past few years. Two years ago I graduated from college and got married, and several months later David left home for college. This past summer my husband and I moved to another state, and Jonathan's high-school graduation is almost upon us. It has definitely been a strange time, a time of adjustment for our family as we have tried to remain close even across many miles.

Alexandra celebrated her thirteenth birthday several months ago, and her birthday present from my parents was a pair of plane tickets so that she could come visit Kevin and me. We had the time of our lives, watching movies, going ice skating, braiding our hair, and just talking nonstop about life. The highlight of the trip came that Saturday night, when David and his girlfriend drove in for a birthday dinner. I had not laughed that hard or felt so relaxed in months. That night I realized that no matter where I move or how mature I think I become, my siblings are still my favorite people in the world (other than my husband, of course). We share precious memories and a uniquely insane sense of humor. I will fight to remain close to them for the rest of my life.

Parents, teach your children to love and appreciate one another now, and help them build memories together. The tears and toil you invest today will yield memories, laughter and love to savor for a lifetime.

What About Dating?

10

Elizabeth

"You need a boyfriend!" "There is no life without dating!" "Sexy is cool!" These were the messages screaming from each page of a misdirected teen magazine I recently received in the mail. Preteens and young teens are aware enough of the opposite sex, thanks to chaotic pubescent hormones. Then on top of these inner impulses, our world conditions them to be absolutely obsessed with dating. They face an onslaught of worldly messages about love and dating everywhere they turn: magazines, teen-oriented television shows and movies, popular music, their friends. No wonder they are boy-crazy and girl-crazy!

It's not just worldly teens who are like this—the world's attitudes can seep into the hearts of "kingdom kids" as well. Even in many of our preteen and teen ministries, young men and women can be boy- or girl-crazy. It seems that all they think and talk about is who likes whom, who is going out with whom, who is cute, who said what about whom to whom...and we wonder why they seem shallow and disinterested in spiritual matters!

Teach Them 'Not Yet'

The battle with worldliness is perhaps the most dangerous and pervasive struggle our young teens must face. Christian parents must teach their children how to think about the opposite gender, dating and love, or they risk losing them to worldliness. In my mind the most important message parents must teach their children was summed up by Solomon thousands of years ago:

> "Daughters of Jerusalem, I charge you
>   by the gazelles and by the does of
>   the field:
> Do not arouse or awaken love
>   until it so desires." (Song of Songs 3:5)

We must teach our children, preteens and young teens to wait for love, to avoid becoming overly concerned with falling in love. In short, our message must be "Not yet."

In many cases, such teaching may need to begin well before the preteen years. The frenzy can begin even in elementary school. Watching my little sister grow up, I was amazed at how much the dating craze already pervaded her kindergarten class. All of her five-year-old classmates and friends were caught up in liking people and "going together." I remember many talks my mother had with Alexandra, teaching her how to think about boys. Mom's teaching gave Alexandra a way out when her friends tried to pressure her to like people or to engage in boy-crazy talk. Alexandra would simply respond, "It's not time for me to get into that yet. I'm too young." Had Mom not addressed these things so forthrightly and consistently even then, by the time Alex reached her preteens, who knows how boy-crazy she would have been.

Some children seem to have a natural attraction to the opposite sex from an early age, and it is especially important for their parents to train them early to change their thinking. Although these attractions are "natural," I have seen parents who constantly ask their children who they like and make their response either a big joke or an issue of great significance. It is not cute or funny for young children or preteens to be completely boy-crazy or girl-crazy. Know that if you encourage this attitude, you quite likely will have a real problem on your hands in the future.

While some children are naturally attracted to the opposite gender, many others are not necessarily interested in dating. However, they may try to become so in order to be cool and fit in with their friends. The pressure they feel to be obsessed with dating is intense. For many children, it is actually a tremendous relief when their parents take the dating pressure off them. They do not want to be boy-crazy or girl-crazy, and so their parents' discipling can give them the escape route they need from the world's pressures. Then they can feel free to just be young and innocent—as God intended them to be.

I am appalled at the way the world blatantly conditions our preteens and young teens to be sexual. The clothing styles for girls, modeled everywhere by their music, television and Hollywood heroines, are embarrassingly immodest. Mothers, it is up to you to take a stand and teach your daughters that they can look beautiful and dress cool without trying to be sexy. Teach them God's standards of purity and modesty from such passages as 1 Timothy 2:9-10 and Ephesians 5:3. And do not be naive as your daughters hit puberty and begin to develop physically; some of the cute outfits they could wear as girls may no longer be appropriate as young women. Believe it or not, young men may find your "little girl" sexy, so be aware of the changes in her body, and help her dress and carry herself appropriately.

It is also important that we teach preteens how to relate to the opposite gender without flirting. Coyness and teasing are "skills" that preteens can pick up surprisingly early. Parents must be on the lookout for such behaviors without becoming paranoid or overbearing.

I realize that there is no way to completely keep your children from liking the opposite sex; and I am not advocating that you should attempt to do so. Of course teens are going to notice and be attracted to the opposite sex—that is a healthy and normal thing! But as with everything in life and in parenting, there is a proper balance. Some parents can overreact in fear and paranoia, and put unfair expectations on their teens: "Because you are young, you should never like anyone. You just need to completely forget about the opposite sex."

I remember vividly my own awakening interest in boys—I suddenly forgot all about the "cooties" and found guys to be quite fascinating. Upon coming home from my first day of high school, one of the first things I told my mom was, "I never knew there were so many cute boys." There was nothing wrong per se with my awakening awareness, and nothing wrong with my beginning to notice certain young men in particular.

However, as each child in our family reached this stage in life, my parents helped us to deal with our changing feelings in a godly way. They never forbade our liking anyone or feeling attracted to anyone— how foolish and unrealistic that would have been. They simply taught us that while it is okay to notice people and think they are good-looking, and even to have one person who we might like above the rest, we should not become obsessed with it. And they taught us from an early age, well before we ever became preteens, that the people we should be interested in were those who loved God as we did.

Another important lesson was about sexual purity in actions and thoughts. They taught us that physical involvement was wrong, but they also did a good deal of teaching about lust. Every one of us began struggling with lust in some way, and along with those struggles came intense guilt, often accompanied by paranoia. We tended to think that every time we noticed an attractive person, we had given in to lust. Mom and Dad had to teach us exactly what lust was and what it was not. They taught that lust is not noticing an attractive person or having some momentary, involuntary physical response (e.g., your stomach knots up when he or she walks by). Lust is deliberately admiring a person's physique, especially focusing on sexual areas of their body. Lust is picturing how someone would look without his or her clothes on and fantasizing about kissing or committing sexual acts (Matthew

5:27-30). This distinction helped free us from the guilt that can plague young teens as they experience sexual struggles for the first time.

Teach Whom to Date

As we became old enough to feel attracted to people, our parents' teaching about whom we should and shouldn't like or date became more specific. There was no panic or pressure in these conversations. They didn't rant, "If you like someone who doesn't go to church, one day you're going to end up falling into sexual sin and leaving God!" Rather, they gave a clear and calm teaching of the way God looks at dating and marriage. I always understood (from a passage like 2 Corinthians 6:14) that I should marry a disciple and that I would ultimately marry one of the young men I dated—hence I should only date godly people.

Once I became a disciple and was old enough to actually start going on dates, I honestly did not want to date guys in the world. Even when I was in teen ministry situations where there were no guys at all or no guys to whom I was attracted, my convictions remained steadfast: I wanted to date and one day marry a man who loved God.

That's not to say that I never struggled at all with being attracted to worldly guys. There were times throughout my preteen and teen years when I would notice guys at school and be attracted to them and even feel tempted to seek their attention. But my parents created such an open atmosphere that I could always be honest about those feelings and struggles without fearing an overreaction from them. My conscience would prick me, and I was always open immediately. I tended to feel so guilty that I would become hyperaware of every feeling or thought I had toward the guy, and this awareness would only make me struggle more every time I was around him. I still remember several times when my mother helped me work through such temptations. She would remind me that what I wanted was a man who loved God above all else, and she urged me to be patient and to think spiritually. She also suggested that I share my faith with him. Doing that always helped me because when he was not interested in God, I would lose interest in him.

It is one thing for a preteen or teen to occasionally be mildly attracted to someone in the world, but if this is a repeated occurrence, then there is definitely cause for alarm. When preteens and teens (even those who are not yet disciples) are consistently falling for people who are not spiritually minded, the parents need to start doing some serious discipling as well as seeking urgent help from the teen ministry leaders. If a teen is deceitful in dating someone, then serious measures may need to be taken. Such teens are in grave danger of walking away from God altogether. In a situation like this, some parents are tempted to react in panic and fear, while others do not respond half as strongly as they should. Involving teen leaders is most helpful because they can be more objective than the parents, and they can provide invaluable experience and insight.

Even when my brothers and I expressed interest in someone who was a disciple, our parents helped us to think spiritually about our attraction. They urged us to consider not simply whether or not the person was the cutest or coolest one in the teen ministry, but whether or not their friendship would bring us closer to God. Again, this helped us avoid becoming boy- or girl-crazy even as disciples in the teen ministry.

Teach How to Date

Teens are ready to date at different points. Most Christian parents allow their teens to begin dating once they become disciples, and in general I think that is a good approach. However, in some cases it may be wise to hold your children off from dating to allow them to mature a little, even if they are already Christians. I was baptized in the spring of my eighth grade year and began dating soon thereafter; however, I wish I had waited at least until I began high school. I was still too immature and insecure when I began dating, and my first date was a rather traumatic experience. I remember being so stiff that I could barely say anything the entire night, and coming home that night wailing, "I never want to go on another date ever again!"[1]

It would have helped if someone had taught me exactly how dates were conducted. I should have known to let my date open doors for me, that it was okay to let him pay for me and how to keep a conversation going, but somehow I was clueless! I did not do much better on my second date. I repeatedly offended my date by either getting out of the car on my own or locking him out. It gets worse. I walked into a pole, discovered a hair on my nachos at the ever high-class Taco Bell, and concluded the glorious evening by stumbling over a tuxedo left on the floor inside the doorway of my house...and with my date accidentally shutting the door on my foot.

Believe it or not, I eventually did get the hang of the dating thing, and I actually started enjoying it. I even "fell in love" when I was fifteen. My brother David and I both had lasting relationships with special people during our high-school years. I had an interest in a disciple for about a year and a half, while my brother had a special friendship with a girl that lasted for several years (and has now turned into a steady dating relationship in college). During that time, my parents felt great about our relationships since both of us had chosen people who were strong disciples and who helped us to remain close to God. They simply urged us to not only enjoy the giddiness and goopiness of liking someone, but to also seek a spiritual depth and a true friendship in our relationships as they progressed.

Even though David and I both had long-term special relationships during our teen years, neither one of us ever dated steady—that is, we never had an official boyfriend or girlfriend. That was thanks to the guidance of our parents. I realize that some teen ministries and parents encourage teens to steady date, and that is fine; it is a decision that every teen, parent and teen ministry are entitled to make on their own. Some teens may do better if they have a steady boyfriend or girlfriend; others are not mature enough to handle it. I personally appreciate my parents' decision not to allow us to steady date in high school. At the time, I did want to call my "friend" my boyfriend, but in the end my parents' decision proved right for me. I had the best of both worlds: I had a special relationship, and we both knew we liked each other, but we could also date other people. In the end, we were spared from breaking each other's hearts by our fickle teenage emotions.

Teach Friendship

The key lesson that will protect preteens and young teens from becoming obsessed with dating is that of simple friendship. So many teens know only extremes in relationships with the opposite sex: either they are not friends and do not talk at all, or they are madly in love (and still may not talk at all!). They are completely awkward and uncomfortable in simple conversation and friendship. Girls flirt, giggle or group in corners to gossip; guys tease, torture or become tongue-tied as they mumble and stare at the floor. Parents, help your children relate to members of the opposite sex! But urge them to focus their efforts on guys and girls in the teen ministry; the truth is, it is very difficult for teens to maintain just a friendship with someone in the world. Somewhere along the way, the lines between friendship and liking tend to blur, setting your child up for an unnecessary struggle. But in the church, guys and girls can learn to be good friends without being "in love" with each other, and such relationships will prepare your teen to one day develop a healthy dating relationship—a relationship built on true friendship as well as attraction.

∿

My parents taught me all these lessons not by preaching at me or launching into boring, rehearsed diatribes, but rather through our everyday conversations about life. My mother took advantage of conversations in which I shared my feelings about a particular guy or about dating in general, and taught me how to think about such matters. Her sincere interest and sense of humor about such things led me to enjoy sharing the fun details of my dating life with her and to seek her input.

Dating can be scary ground for both teens and their parents, but it does not have to be a subject of conflict or turmoil. With the Bible, wise counsel and guidelines to help you along, you can successfully navigate your way through the ups and downs of teenage dating...without strangling or otherwise harming your child (or their prospective dates) and without standing on the front porch, rifle in hand. You may even end up with some great, and probably hilarious, memories to recall and to share.

NOTES

1. Read my book *Glory Days* to get the full story on my early dating woes: (Billerica, Mass.: Discipleship Publications International, 1999) 49-70.

The 'Difficult' Child

11

Geri

I can do everything through him who gives
me strength.

Philippians 4:13

We have raised four children, and despite what
you might think, not one of them could be labeled "an
easy child." Raising each one has had its own special
challenges and has taken all of the wisdom, energy,
patience and prayer that we had to give. So, at some
point each of our children was "difficult" to raise.

However, there do seem to be some children who
present greater challenges than most. Raising them
can be like a ride on a never-ending roller coaster!
They excite and thrill us, yet they exhaust and exas-
perate us, anger and confuse us. Though we love
them with all our hearts, they can cause us to question everything that we know and believe. They can
also destroy our confidence as people and as parents.
One thing you must never forget: you are the parent,
the God-given caretaker and authority in your children's lives. Although they may not show it, you are

still the most important person in their world, and they desperately need you. Parents, you have a job to do, and you must rise to its challenges with courage and confidence. You can do this...with God!

THE WITHDRAWN CHILD

There is nothing more discouraging in a family than a sullen, withdrawn child. He or she is capable of casting a dark shadow over everyone and can destroy the atmosphere within minutes of walking into a room. We have probably all experienced this "adolescent phenomenon," and yet when it is our own child in our own family it is even more disheartening.

Some children come into the world with personalities that are more introverted. They are more reserved and more easily intimidated. They are happiest by themselves and often do not seem to need people at all. As they reach the early teen years, riddled with insecurities and bouts of self-consciousness, their inability to express themselves is even more pronounced. They become increasingly aloof and downright rude. As parents our job is to take the children that God has given us and help them become all that God wants them to be. They may never be "life of the party" kids, but they must become people who relate well and bond deeply with others. What are some things we can do to help the withdrawn adolescent?

1. Expect Friendliness

My early teen years were marked by timidity and awkwardness. It is amazing that to this day the memories of that time in my life can still bring back such feelings of fear and insecurity. I will forever be grateful for my mother's determination that I not use shyness as an excuse for rudeness. She insisted that I speak when spoken to and that I look people "in the eyes" rather than look at the floor or into the distance. I vividly remember being taught how to shake hands, not like a "limp dishrag," but firmly and warmly.

There are some things that are just right, and we as parents must be dogged in our determination to teach them to our children. Warmth, friendliness and respect—these are things that must be expected regardless of a person's natural temperament. You may have expected these things when your children were young. Now that they are young teens, continue to expect them even more so. It is amazing how the basics of social graces can encourage even the most timid to change.

2. Find Some Common Ground

Trying to get a sullen adolescent to talk to you can be frustrating and next to impossible, especially if we try too hard. Often the best way to draw out a withdrawn child is to just spend time together in a relaxed setting rather than sitting across a table focusing on the need to talk.

Find something that your son or daughter likes to do and do it together. Lasting relationships are forged by shared experiences and memories. Fishing, hunting, sports, shopping, car trips—doing enjoyable things like these together will often "loosen the tongue" as nothing else can.

Of our four children, David as a young man was often the one who would hold things in. Sam realized that it seldom worked when he pushed him to talk. He learned the invaluable lesson of "play first, talk later." He found that if he spent time in the backyard throwing the football to David, they could then sit on the back steps and David would start talking. It took a lot of time devoted to doing things with David to help him relax and open up. As the years have gone by, not only do they have an incredibly close friendship, but also David has learned to express his thoughts and his feelings with his dad and with other people.

3. Listen to What They Do Say

Why is it that some children talk all the time, telling much more than you really need to know, while other children say so little?

If you are the parent of one of those "silent types," it is so important to listen carefully to them. They may say less but often what they do tell you is very insightful and pointed. Sometimes they are putting a little bit out there, testing the waters to see if it is really safe to tell you more. Listen to them. Really hear what they are saying to you and respond accordingly.

Our young teens will say many things that seem to us to be immature or rash or just completely wrong. Even if you must disagree or correct them, do so with respect. A child who feels constantly "put down" or "jumped on" whenever he opens his mouth will become only more withdrawn and angry. You cannot correct every single thing they say. Just as you had to do when they were toddlers...choose your battles! Also, watch your tone of voice. Is it harsh or sarcastic? Are your words belittling? Our children need much direction and teaching from us, yet they also need to feel respected. Not listening or not respecting will only drive them away at a time in their lives when they need us the most.

> Fathers, do not exasperate your children; instead, bring them up in the training and instruction of the Lord. (Ephesians 6:4)

4. Deal with the Hurts and Disappointments of Life

Some of you are dealing with children who are aloof and unexpressive, not because they have always been this way, but because they have been deeply hurt by life. Not only are you suffering for your child, but you may feel a tremendous sense of guilt yourself. Perhaps there has been a divorce or death, physical or sexual abuse. These are things that can shake the very foundation of a child's life. Some will become defiant and outwardly angry while others will draw within themselves and grieve alone. Whatever the situation is, hurts, sins, mistakes and failures in life must be dealt with and faced, or they will forever cast a shadow over their lives.

Address the things that you know have caused the hurt. Sometimes our children have been hurt deeply by other people and situations that are completely out of our control. We must help them to talk about their feelings, to face the situations and to overcome the anger and bitterness that can come into their hearts.

Probably the most difficult situation is when our children are hurting as a result of our own sins and failures. You may be hurting so badly yourself that you don't feel able to help anyone else, or your own guilt is so great that it has taken away your confidence as a parent. You must face your own life with tremendous humility and courage. Get right with God yourself; let strong disciples into your life to help you. Deeply accept God's grace. You may need to apologize to your children. Do it with sincerity and humility, allowing them to fully open up their own hearts and express the hurt you have caused them. When we as parents are vulnerable like this, our children usually are eager to forgive us.

Probably one of the saddest things Sam and I have had to deal with in our years of being in the ministry has been helping young people overcome their feelings of anger and pain over their parents' divorces. Divorce is not just something that happens between a husband and wife, but it deeply affects children! I am not trying to heap more guilt on some of you for things that have already happened in the past, but I am urging you if at all possible, to fix your marriages and with God's help, make them great. If it is too late to do that, help your children. Don't be afraid to let them talk to you about how these things have affected their lives.

Lastly, understand that parents are not perfect people, yet we have been entrusted with the most important job in the world. Regardless of the mistakes you have made in the past, you cannot, must not abdicate your position as parent, nor can you allow your children to use your past failures as an excuse to become bitter or manipulative. They desperately need you to learn from your past, but they just as desperately need you to be a strong parent who will guide their lives in the direction they need to go.

THE DEFIANT CHILD

I think the most frightening situation that we may find ourselves in as parents is living under the same roof with a child who has become defiant and rebellious. We can feel so powerless and confused. We hurt for them, but we can also be so angered by their behavior. This book especially addresses raising preteens and younger teens—children who are still very much under a parent's authority. There does come a time with older teens when you have done all you can do for them, and life and God himself will have to further discipline your child. But these younger ones can be dealt with—and must be. You have a limited time to reach them, so be urgent yet calmly confident. The following are some principles that I encourage you to put into practice as you raise your child.

1. Disrespectful Talk Is Unacceptable

I am shocked at the way so many parents allow their children to speak to them. The tone of voice, the expression on their faces, the sarcastic remarks and the outright disrespect are appalling. Much of this defiance as teenagers is because of disrespect that was allowed when they were younger. Decide that you will no longer allow this kind of behavior.

Several things can be done to break the sinful habit of disrespectful talk. If your teen speaks to you with an ugly tone of voice, if he or she starts

arguing with you (arguing is different from respectfully asking you to reconsider), or if he or she reacts
angrily or defiantly—end the discussion! In our
house anything that is asked for with a defiant,
contemptuous attitude will be absolutely, automatically given a resounding "No"! It may take a few
skirmishes, but if you are determined never to be
swayed by disrespect, your children will learn that
for practical reasons, if for no other, disrespect does
not pay. The key here is to stand your ground. Do
not allow yourself to continually be drawn into
"word battles" with a twelve-year-old. If you are not
careful, you will sound like adolescents arguing
with each other; you will have stooped to his or her
level of immaturity and have lost not only the
battle, but the respect of your child as well. You are
not the child. You are the parent, and God has
commanded that you be obeyed and respected:

> Children, obey your parents in the Lord, for
> this is right. (Ephesians 6:1)

2. Parents Work Together

As mentioned in chapter 4, "Two are better than
one," and nowhere is this principle more true than
when raising a rebellious child. It will take the
insight, wisdom and determination of both parents
working together to guide this one through the turbulent teenage years. By yourself, you may be too
weak, too overbearing, too unnerved or too confused.
But, working together, you can stand firm and strong.
Each of you will provide perspective and insight that
is invaluable, but you also will have your own areas
of weakness and blindness. When you work together,

complementing and completing each other, you will certainly be "smarter" and better parents.

3. Discipline by Applying Appropriate Consequences

One of the reasons parents are often unsuccessful in dealing with rebellious and defiant children is that they do not know how to make the punishment truly "fit the crime." Often we fuss, yell, lecture and then issue a punishment, but the true recipient of the discipline becomes the parent or the entire family rather than the teen. For example, over and over again I have heard teens talk about being grounded repeatedly for almost everything they do that is wrong. The kids are boasting about being grounded again while I hear the parents whining in misery about the discontented teen who is sulking or complaining twenty-four hours as he sits around the house grounded. What is wrong with this picture? The parents are miserable and the teen is as defiant as ever! If you find yourself doing the same thing over and over again without any real impact or change in your child, something is wrong with the punishment.

All of life involves consequences. For a punishment to be effective, it has to have some sting to it. It has to be something that is the logical consequence of their undesirable behavior as well as something they do not want to happen again. A discipline is effective when it brings about a change of behavior.

Let me give you a couple of examples of appropriate discipline that produced change. A close friend of our family was having some real challenges with their son as he reached the middle-school years. He began to be very deceitful and defiant, even bragging to the kids at school when he was in trouble with his parents or his teachers. His parents had talks, made threats and confined him to his room, but the young man seemed only to be drawn more and more away from them and into the world.

The parents finally decided to get very firm and apply consequences that would not be soon forgotten. Since a lot of the problem with this particular boy was his laziness and a desire to be cool at all costs, his dad decided to make the punishments more appropriate. Every time he was deceitful and tried to take the easy way out of something, not only did he have to go back and deal with the situation, but also he was given a hard job to do. Over the last several months he has completely cleaned out their garage, even to the point of learning how to put up shelves on the walls. As new consequences for his behavior have been called for, he has been given other jobs around the house. His parents say that the next one will be organizing their attic (they're almost looking forward to this one!). What began as consequences to laziness and deceit is building in him a strong work ethic and a godly pride in doing things excellently.

We had an incident with our son last year when we had to apply some strong consequences, which would hopefully not soon be forgotten. Jonathan has quite an entertaining sense of humor and a quick wit. He can get everyone around him laughing and having a great time. However, the other side of this "gift" is his tendency to be sarcastic, and he sometimes crosses the line of respect. After several discussions about this, we found out that Jonathan was continuing to joke and carry on in some of his classes, even to the point of being rebuked by several of his teachers.

We decided enough was enough. We told Jonathan how disappointed we were in his lack of maturity as a young man. If he was too immature to know what was respectful and appropriate behavior, then we felt he was too immature to handle some of the other privileges he'd been given, namely the privilege of driving his car. Jonathan was a junior in high school and had an old car that he very proudly drove to school every day. Although the school provided bus transportation to and from school, by the time most of our kids were upperclassmen, they drove cars or rode with one another. In our city the buses were considered definitely for the "young ones." We told Jonathan that he would have to ride the bus for an unspecified period of time and that for everything else he would have to depend on others for rides. Until he was mature enough to control himself in other areas of his life, we would not consider him mature enough to drive.

As if this were not punishment enough, it got worse. Since Jonathan did not usually ride the bus (and none of his friends did), he did not know where the bus stop was or what time the bus came in the mornings. We expected him to find this out. Well...as teens often do...he put off finding out until it was too late. The first morning he was to ride the bus, I took him to a place that he "thought" the bus might come, hoping for the best. I left him and went home. God must have thought Jonathan needed a little more discipline if he was to learn his lesson because, in the end, the bus never came. Jonathan walked the entire five or six miles to school, arriving over an hour and a half late. Jonathan was without the use of his car for several weeks, and every day he got on the school bus he was reminded of his childish, disrespectful behavior. It is not one of his most pleasant memories, but the lessons he learned will certainly not be easily forgotten.

4. One Child Should Not Destroy the Atmosphere of the Family

There is truth in the statement, "A parent is no happier than his unhappiest child." We love our children, and when one is not doing well, we can allow that to completely dominate our lives. Many other things may be going well, but we hardly seem to notice because we are so focused on the one child who is having difficulties. Parents must rise to the challenge of dealing calmly and consistently with this one while still enjoying and guiding the rest of the family. If you have other children, they need you too. They need to know they are a part of a family that still laughs and talks and enjoys one another. Too many times I have seen children withdraw because no matter how hard they try to be the good kid, Mom and Dad only seem to be aware of the one who is causing problems. Hard as this may be, you've got to rise above the worry and fears and still be there for the others who also need you.

5. Be Willing to Do Whatever It Takes

Don't you wish that you could quickly straighten out a rebellious child with a hard talk and some strong discipline? Sometimes that may be all it takes, but often a young teen who has become defiant is not going to be easily turned around. As parents, we must do whatever is needed to help our children make the changes they need to make.

One of the things that parents must deal with as their children grow older is the influence of their peers. The desire for acceptance becomes overpowering and is either a positive motivation or a negative one, depending on the kinds of friends they are surrounded by. If your son or daughter is becoming rebellious, deceitful or increasingly worldly, check out the friends he or she is spending time with. The Bible says, "Do not be misled: 'Bad company corrupts good character'" (1 Corinthians 15:33).

We have often encouraged parents whose teens are not doing well to move to another neighborhood or town where there is a group of spiritual teens who will be a positive influence on their children. These friendships can strengthen them to withstand the pressures of conformity and will give them a sense of belonging. I can think of countless families who have made these moves for the sake of their children. One family moved across town out of concern for their son who was in some unhealthy relationships and was becoming increasingly rebellious. He was not doing well in school, was not getting along with his teachers, and was becoming more and more alienated from his parents and uninterested in spiritual things. Against his will they moved down the street from another family of disciples with boys his age who were strong enough to have a positive influence on him. I will never forget the joy his parents expressed—and that we all shared—as we watched this kid begin to relax, let teen disciples in and then become a Christian himself. I believe his parents moved just in time. Had they waited even a few more months, it might have been too late.

We had another family move into the area from a large church up north just as their daughter was finishing middle school. They moved into a suburban area where the schools were good and they could afford a house for their young family. However, there were no other disciples' kids in her school. A year or so later as their daughter began high school, we all became concerned at her lack of spiritual growth and her emotional distance from her parents and spiritual friends in the church. I was impressed when her parents decided to move to a nearby town where there was a strong group of teen disciples in the same high school. Because houses were more expensive there, the family moved into an apartment. Several months after they made the move we all were thrilled as her parents baptized her into Christ with a large group of her teen friends cheering her on. This family sacrificed the "American Dream" so their daughter would be saved. God blessed them with the "Parent's Dream." They decided they wanted a family and a real home more than they wanted a nice house and yard.

There are other ways that parents do whatever it takes to help their children. I will never forget the year I was fifteen and becoming increasingly defiant. My parents sent me away to spend the summer with people who could be a positive, healthy influence in my life. I came back a very different young lady.

I also think of the weeks that my own children have spent at the Atlanta Church Camp (The Swamp). It cost money and was a long drive down and back, but it has been worth every bit of effort because of the ways this experience has helped mold my children into the people they are today.

It takes time, sacrifice, devotion and a lot of faith to help our children through the hard times. I urge you to do whatever it takes—it is worth it.

THE SELFISH CHILD

I find myself more and more concerned about a particular "difficult child" who often goes unaddressed—that is the selfish child. While the very nature of most children is to be selfish, there must come a time when they begin to put their own wants and desires aside for the sake of others and for what is right and good. Too many of our children are not transitioning out of selfish immaturity and self-centeredness. Perhaps it is because here in America, our children are growing up in a time of unprecedented peace and prosperity. It may also be that in our desire to love our children and be great parents, we have actually fostered a deep selfishness in them. Many of them feel they deserve the blessings of their lives, believing them to be some of their "unalienable rights."

I believe that one of the reasons many teenagers, as well as adults, are discouraged and depressed is because they have never learned the lessons of unselfishness. Jesus said it so well in Luke 9:24-25: "For whoever wants to save his life will lose it, but whoever loses his life for me will save it. What good is it for a man to gain the whole world, and yet lose or forfeit his very self?" What are some of the things we can do to help our children become less selfish?

1. Talk About It

All of the Laing children have had to deal with the sin of selfishness, but it was most evident in our youngest children. Often in families where there are a number of children, the "babies" become especially self-centered. For years they have been doted upon by brothers and sisters, Mom and Dad. They are cute and entertaining, the apple of the family's eye. If ever they need or want something, someone is there to provide it. As they grow older, what was once so adorable becomes ugly and demanding. Decide that as a parent you do not want your children to grow up to be selfish, demanding adults who have tantrums or sulk when they don't get their way. We don't want our children to be so self-centered that they cannot get along with spouses, their employers or friends.

Talk often about the importance of giving to others and considering their feelings and needs. Sometimes the talks will be serious conversations in which you sit down and open the Bible. We've studied with our children scriptures such as 1 Corinthians 13, the great chapter on love, and Philippians 2, Paul's great admonishment for us to be selfless like Jesus.

Point out to your children the times when they are being pushy, demanding or selfish. Talk about ways their behavior hurts other people and even drives others away from them. Young teens deeply want to be liked and to be close to people, yet they are often completely oblivious to the things they are doing that are so offensive to other people. Our job as parents is to teach our children how to relate to those around them in a way that is loving and kind. At the same time we need to help them stand strong in the areas of moral righteousness.

A couple came to us asking for help with their daughter, the youngest of three children. This twelve-year-old was driving Mom, Dad and her siblings crazy! One minute she was sullen and pouty, the next she was loud and bossy. Although the youngest and smallest, her moods controlled and dominated the household. Her parents own feelings for her fluctuated from complete frustration and anger to feeling sorry for her. We encouraged them to have a strong talk with their daughter, showing her who she was becoming and how she was hurting the entire family. They were kind, but they were very honest and straightforward about her selfishness and how ugly it was. They also told her that her behavior was no longer acceptable and would be dealt with if it continued. She cried and for the first time began to accept responsibility for her actions. She still occasionally falls back into old ways, but her parents are firm in their resolve to not allow her or their family be dominated by her self-centeredness.

We have had so many of these talks with our children. Sometimes we wondered if we were being heard at all. It has helped me to remember the things my mother constantly talked to me about—things I am sure she thought I was not hearing and yet even today echo in my mind and my conscience. Not too long ago, as I was dropping Alexandra off at a party, I opened my mouth to issue the usual admonitions about her behavior. Before a word came out she said, "I know, mom...don't talk too much, don't be bossy and do my best to think about other people." Keep talking; they are listening!

2. Teach Them to Be Responsible

One of the reasons so many of our young people are selfish and immature is because we do too much for them. It is hard, exhausting work to run a household and care for a family. But it is often harder than it needs to be because good-hearted, well-meaning parents carry the entire burden themselves. You do your children no favor when you shield them from the hard work of living life. We told our children years ago that having a larger family is lots of fun, but it also means lots of work...and everyone must help. Large family or small, you must expect your children to help with the daily chores of running a home. Give them jobs to do—and expect them to be done well. Not only will they learn to be hard workers and responsible, but they will also grow in their confidence and in their ability to handle the pressures and responsibilities of life.

Another area where we must expect our children to work diligently is with their schoolwork. I am amazed at the pressure so many parents put on themselves to sit down and do their children's homework with them. You are wearing yourselves out! Not only is there tension as you are constantly pushing and prodding your child to pay attention and work harder, but in a strange way you are taking the responsibility off him or her, where it should be, and putting it on yourself. When you are there, pushing or helping, your child will not feel the personal burden to figure it out. I genuinely believe that while you are trying to produce a good student, you may actually be encouraging laziness or inhibiting self-confidence.

We never have done homework with our children. We may quiz them for a vocabulary test (after they have studied) or answer a question if they are really stuck, but we will not be their excuse to be lazy-minded. As they have gotten older, I don't think I could help much if I tried. But more importantly, it is their responsibility, and I do not want to rob them of the hard work that is part of the learning process.

3. Give Them Opportunities to Serve

I do not think anything has helped our children with their selfishness more than the times they have spent helping other people. One of the reasons so many teens are consumed with themselves is because they honestly do not realize how much they have been given. Encourage your children to serve those who have needs.

All three of our older children have been able to go to third-world countries with HOPE Youth Corps and have spent time working with the poor and especially with orphans. Each time they have come back with softer hearts and a much deeper appreciation for all they have been given. When Elizabeth went to Africa, she befriended a young teen disciple who had been repeatedly molested by members of her family. She realized that the problems and struggles she had in her life were nothing compared to what this young girl faced every day. When David went to Romania, he became close to a thirteen-year-old orphan and his little sister. He played with him, talked to him and read the Bible with him.

When the day came for them to say goodbye, the little boy who was so hardened by the hurts of life, hugged David, buried his head into his shoulder and wept. I'll never forget David's tears as he told us about him after he returned home.

This past summer Jonathan was able to go with HOPE Youth Corps to Kingston, Jamaica. I think he probably worked harder than he had ever worked in his life. He was part of a drama troop that prepared a musical presentation designed to teach children and performed it for several orphanages. They served in the orphanages by painting and cleaning and, most of all, by reaching out to and loving children who had no families. When Jonathan came home, he was determined not to forget what he had seen and experienced. He wanted to do something to help the children in Jamaica. He remembered how few of them had shoes, so he decided to ask people in America for their used shoes to send to Jamaica. He collected over 1,300 pairs of shoes!

Our kids do not have to go to another country to serve people who are less fortunate. There are people with needs all around us—most of us are just so unaware. Alexandra and her preteen group at church have had their eyes opened and their hearts softened as they have helped in soup kitchens and visited homes for the elderly.

Our children are so blessed, but until they see how many people are not as fortunate and until they experience the joy and satisfaction of making someone else's life a little better, they will not understand or appreciate all that they have. Our children will overcome selfishness when they learn to give themselves away!

Perhaps the title of this chapter could be "Raising Children Is a Difficult Task." All of our children come into the world with unique abilities and strengths, but they also have particular weaknesses that, left undealt with, will only become more pronounced and ultimately can ruin their lives. As parents we must raise all of our children to become all that God desires for them to be, developing the good and overcoming the bad. The withdrawn child can learn to deeply love people, to be a loyal and devoted friend. The rebellious child can learn not only to respect authority but also to channel his or her strong will and become one who accomplishes great things in life. The selfish child can become a person of compassion and care for others, living a life of fulfillment instead of shallowness and emptiness.

Raising every child has its challenges and difficulties, but nothing is so satisfying as watching your children change and mature into the strong, young adults that God envisioned when he made them and entrusted them to us.

12

Sam

Over the last few years, there has been an amazing increase in the diagnoses of childhood psychological disorders. Along with this has come a skyrocketing proliferation of psychoactive drugs prescribed for young children, Ritalin being the most common. How are we as disciples of Jesus to regard this? Does it have substance, or is it a product of worldly thinking?

Committed disciples, including those with training in medicine and psychology, have different perspectives on this matter. However, in communicating with others, I have found one key area of agreement: *There has been an incredible, nationwide misuse and over-prescription of stimulant medications.* This is not to say that there is never a situation in which a child legitimately needs medicinal help to restore proper chemical balance in his or her system. But, I am concerned that some disciples are buying too quickly into this approach without a great deal of thought and could be harming their children in the process. My intent in this chapter is not to pronounce the final verdict on the use of medication, but to say that before we make the decision, we must realize that a variety of other issues can, and often do, contribute to behavior problems.

Let me open the examination of this topic with several observations.

God's Word, Not Human Wisdom

When the Bible speaks on a subject, it has authority above the wisdom of man. God's word provides all the wisdom and insights we need to successfully live our lives and raise our children. The Bible describes many of the issues and problems children face, and tells us as adults how to deal with them. Worldly psychologists and psychiatrists do not have a spiritual perspective. They often come up with a mistaken cause for the problems and mistaken solutions as well. This is not to say that mental health professionals have no place in helping people, but rather to say that their assessments should not be regarded as infallible medical or scientific authority.[1]

Mental health issues are not as easily defined and diagnosed as other medical problems. Even in the medical field, there is plenty of room for judgment and human error, to which the famous "second opinion" bears witness. How much more, then, should we be cautious in the more uncertain areas of human psychology and emotion, especially when it comes to raising our children! We have seen the fads come and go in the mental health field, and I am concerned that the recent proliferation of the diagnoses of childhood disorders might one day be as outmoded and discredited as some other philosophies that have come through the profession.

Child Problem or Adult Problem?

Some of the diagnoses being handed out may be simply demonstrating that adults are losing patience with children and would rather "drug" them than devote themselves to their upbringing. (My tone is not intended to be harsh here; please stay with me. I just want to get our attention and make sure we are making certain decisions after much soul searching, prayer and advice.) Second, some of the problems of children may be caused by adult behaviors. I will elaborate on this later, but let me say that rarely in history have so many parents been as preoccupied with their jobs and spending so little time to raise their children. Could it be that some of our children's anxieties are brought on by the fact that parents are uninvolved in their lives?

Syntcha Darby, a licensed counselor, recently shared this thought with me:

> In my practice, the doctors often have to fight to get the parents to take responsibility for the training and leadership at home that will help the children flourish. Medication is definitely not appropriate for all children, and not a cure-all for those who need it as an adjunct to parental guidance and training.[2]

While busy adults with many other priorities may hope medication will bring a quick fix to the child's behavior problems, it is more likely that the real solution will come only through a parent who takes responsibility to work with that child until change occurs.

DRAMATIC CHANGES

Our society has undergone unprecedented upheaval in the last fifty years. Dramatic changes have occurred, changes that have deeply altered the fabric of our lives. It is my belief that these changes are affecting our children in a negative way and are behind many of the childhood disorders. I will list below some of these changes.

1. Women in the Workforce

After World War II, women in large numbers began to work outside the home for the first time. This meant that when their children came home from school, there was no one home, or they were sent to day care or to the homes of other people until their parents came home from work. When the mother did come home, she not only had to provide for the needs of her husband and children, but to cope with her weariness as well. There was just not enough of her to go around.

We are now many years deep into raising children in this way. I consider it one of the great tragedies of our time, and one of the most grievous blows to children that has ever been delivered. The Bible teaches clearly that women are "to be busy at home" (Titus 2:5). God's wisdom is proven true when we consider that it is incredibly difficult for women to care for the needs of their husbands and children and hold down a demanding job. Certainly there are situations in which a mother's working outside the home is unavoidable. She must trust that God will take care of the children if she is seeking to do the very best she can. But whatever their life situations, mothers need to realize the importance of nurturing their children.

Much of the anxiety and nervousness of some children could be attributed to the lack of "mothering" they are receiving. Children need the attention and care their mother provides to help them face their difficulties and challenges. Nothing replaces time spent with Mom. To go out into the world of school and play, children need to feel the uncompromised support of their mothers. How much of our children's anxieties and anger now being treated with medication could be resolved if they simply had more of their mothers' attention? If moms genuinely have to work outside the home, I would encourage them to search for ways to carve out more time with their children.[3]

2. Divorce and Marriage Problems

The divorce rate has skyrocketed in the last fifty years. More and more children are now being raised by single parents or in broken homes. The Bible says that "God hates divorce" (Malachi 2:16). Divorce is devastating to children. It can hamper and even destroy their ability to trust, to love, to build meaningful relationships and to be happy. So-called experts tried to tell us it wouldn't matter, that divorce would not hurt our children, but they were wrong—dead wrong, as prominent social scientists are now admitting.[4] We are raising a generation of kids who struggle terribly with building relationships and making lifetime commitments. Children who live in a home full of arguing, fighting and tension are not going to do well in school. We can say that they have a brain disorder, but might the real problem be that they are upset about the disorder in their lives? Is it any surprise that such children are angry, anxious and unfocused?

3. Absent or Weak Father

The number of children born out of wedlock has increased in monumental proportions. Combining this with the divorce rate, we have huge numbers of children who are not raised with a meaningful male influence. The Bible gives to the father the role of nurturing, training and instructing (Ephesians 6:4). Without a strong, forceful and secure male presence children grow up without moorings. No matter how strong a woman is, there is the need for a solid and powerful male presence in the life of a child.[5] Many children are growing up without the benefit of firm discipline by a father. They come into our school systems and are not accustomed to dealing with authority. They act up and they act out. As a result, they are diagnosed as having a brain disorder and are put on medication when their real problem is that they simply have never been properly disciplined.

4. The Digital Age

We are in the midst of a breathtaking revolution brought on by technology. We live in a new world of videos, television, cell phones and computers. From birth our children are bombarded with images on television and sounds from headsets or speakers. I spoke with a pediatric neurosurgeon from Duke University concerning this, and his assessment was fascinating. He noted that this kind of information coming into a young, developing brain affects the way the brain responds to stimuli. Defining it as a "hard wiring problem," he observed that children who spend hours in front of the television or computer screen are likely to be frustrated in a classroom. They are accustomed to constantly changing images and stimulation, and when the teacher becomes the least bit boring or repetitive, they are going to become fidgety. They are discontent because they cannot control the classroom situation. He said he knew that some of his colleagues would disagree with him, but that was his assessment.

While the scientific research on this is yet to be done, I have to believe that this conclusion is accurate. Our children constantly watch television, DVDs and videos, and play rapid-fire video games. When they are not doing that, they are listening to their CD players. So much information and cacophony is being pumped into their brains that they are on overload. Add to this their power to manipulate the information at their whim, and we understand why they become impossible to deal with in other situations. The solution is not to put them on drugs to help them focus, but to wisely monitor their involvement in the digital world.

5. A Sedentary Lifestyle

Physical education and recess are on the way out in most of our school systems and have been for quite some time. Unless they are involved in organized sports, some children get very little exercise. During the school day, children are cooped up in classrooms. (At my daughter's middle school, they have four minutes to change classes.) Kids have no opportunity to go outside and blow off excess energy. No wonder they are nervous and fidgety!

Most children come home and retreat into their rooms to watch television or play video games rather than go outdoors to play. In the past, children came home and either worked for their parents outdoors or played with other kids in creative games that they made up themselves. This is largely no longer true. Many children, if they do play at all, do so in closely supervised, tightly organized sports leagues. This is hardly the fun, enjoyable and carefree life that children once enjoyed. For many children, sports are just another form of pressure. Why don't we permit them to be children again, and let them go out under the clear blue sky and have a little fun?

6. Pressure from Parents

Parents are increasingly pushing their children in academics and athletics. It seems that the pressure to do well in school has increased immensely in the last few years. Parents are often concerned about getting their children into the best private schools and then into the best colleges. They therefore pressure their children to do extremely well in school and to take on the extra projects that will spruce up their college applications. Children are living with responsibilities of adults when they are still young and needing time to enjoy life. Even in sports events, parents are more concerned that their children excel and win rather than simply go out, do their best and have a good time. No wonder our children are experiencing emotional and mental meltdown!

7. Schedule Upheaval

With our increasing mobility has come increasing chaos in our family lives. Parents are commuting farther to work and are spending more time away overnight. Schools are offering more activities for children after school hours. Rarely do families have the time to sit down and have a nice family meal—they are too scattered. Parents are not home many evenings with their children to help them get to bed or to ensure that they have a consistent bedtime. The result? Nervous, anxious children who cannot control their emotions or their attention.

8. Junk Food

The proliferation of the fast food market is a phenomenon of our time. Unfortunately, fast food is a product of our frenetic lifestyles; with the upheaval of our schedules comes less time eating at home. Fast-food chains are dispensers of high sugar, high fat and often nonnutritious food. Children consuming this diet are getting increasingly out of shape and out of control. They are also becoming obese, which comes with its own set of emotional and mental challenges. The solution is to change their diets and get them eating healthy. Healthy bodies will enable kids to behave, feel and think better.

∿

Even in the mental health community there is controversy about the prescribing of drugs like Ritalin for children. The fact is that these drugs have been used extensively for only a few years. It is impossible at this point to say what the use of

Ritalin and drugs like it will do to the rapidly growing and changing brain of a child. It is time to step back and take a serious look. I would urge you to thoroughly research this and consider differing viewpoints on this crucial subject so that you can make an informed decision.

Our children depend on us for protection. So before we place them on medication, let us think long and hard. I believe the key is to help your child adjust and flourish by first approaching the situation using other methods and giving much parental attention. At some point you may come to the conclusion and conviction that medication is necessary, but I would urge you to take that step cautiously, thoughtfully and prayerfully.

We must live before God with our decisions. I cannot and would not presume to decide this for you. I fully realize that some of my thoughts in this chapter are not based upon scientific research. They are the results of my own observations and are an attempt to apply scriptural principles with common-sense reasoning. Take them for whatever they are worth as the advice of a fellow parent and concerned friend. I can only leave you with the thoughts I have shared in the hope that they may give you some insight into an area that we must weigh with great care as we guide our children through the wonder years.

NOTES

1. I would give the same word of caution to disciples in the mental health field that I give to disciples (myself included!) who attend denominational seminaries: Beware of the allure of worldly thinking and theology!

2. This text was excerpted from a letter written to me by my friend and fellow disciple, Syntcha Darby, M.Ed., LPC, NCC.

3. I recommend that moms read the following two chapters as they evaluate their work and family situation: Sheila Jones, "Deciding Whether to Work Full Time," *Life and Godliness for Everywoman* (Billerica, Mass.: Discipleship Publications International, 2000), 68-77; Loretta Berndt, "Business at Home," *Life and Godliness for Everywoman* (Billerica, Mass.: Discipleship Publications International), 78-82.

4. See Barbara Defoe Whitehead's revealing and now-famous article, "Dan Quayle Was Right," (*Atlantic Monthly*, April 1993). It can be found on the Internet at

http://www.theatlantic.com/politics/family/danquayl.htm.

(Note that there is no "e" after "Quayl" in this address.)

5. I speak here from my own experience. My father died when I was twelve, and the male leadership I lacked as a teen was not provided until I became a disciple at nineteen. It was then that older men in the church began providing much of the needed guidance and discipline in my life, for which I will always be thankful.

Broken and Blended

13

Sam

He predestined us to be adopted as his sons through Jesus Christ, in accordance with his pleasure and will.

> Ephesians 1:5

For he himself is our peace, who has made the two one and has destroyed the barrier, the dividing wall of hostility, by abolishing in his flesh the law with its commandments and regulations. His purpose was to create in himself one new man out of the two, thus making peace, and in this one body to reconcile both of them to God through the cross, by which he put to death their hostility. He came and preached peace to you who were far away and peace to those who were near. For through him we both have access to the Father by one Spirit.

Consequently, you are no longer foreigners and aliens, but fellow citizens with God's people and members of God's household.

> Ephesians 2:14-19

God himself is the father of a broken and blended family, his church. When you consider all the different kinds of people in his family, you realize that God presides over quite a motley group. His children were not raised in the same home; they come from very different backgrounds, and they bring some very serious baggage into the family! God does not give up in despair; he instead uses the difficulty of the situation to teach his children how to love and then holds up his family as his pride and joy.

If you are a parent in a situation like this, know two things: it will not always be easy, and you never have to despair. If you can be realistic and faithful at the same time, you will see some amazing things happen in a situation that is for many others a tragic and heartbreaking occasion of defeat.

The most important factor in this situation is the unifying power of God himself. If God can build a church family with his children, then by imitating him, you too can see incredible progress in bringing your family together. It is God's will for every family to be spiritual and for every parent to depend on him. In a broken or a blended family, spirituality and dependence upon God are all the more crucial if the family unit is to survive and prosper.

Children of Divorce

If you are raising a child who has gone through a divorce, you will need an extra measure of love, patience, compassion and wisdom. The older the child was when the divorce occurred, the deeper the wounds and the more challenging it will be to parent the child. Certainly all children who have gone through the divorce of their parents are feeling many things. It is so important to find out and understand what is going on inside their heads and hearts.

They are hurting. They may not show it outwardly and obviously, but they are hurt. They feel, to one degree or another, abandoned by someone who was supposed to protect them. This can make them wonder if there is something deeply flawed about them. They don't realize that parents usually divorce for personal reasons, not because they dislike their children. Children who feel unloved and unwanted will need much love, yet they may act as if they do not. They might resist any attempt for it to be given them, especially by a stepparent. The hurt they feel can cause them to be deeply unhappy and pessimistic, always seeing the dark side of life, always expecting the worst.

They may be deeply angry. Mixed with the feelings of hurt can be a smoldering anger, an anger that shows itself more clearly as the child matures. As they grow up, they may begin to look more intently at the divorce and start blaming one or both parents for the misery it caused. They may focus their anger on the parent they live with, or on the one who is absent. They may be very angry with a stepparent, who is regarded as a stranger who has come into their lives to make an already difficult situation even worse. And when you add this anger on top of the hurt we described above, you have an even more difficult child to raise.

They are mistrustful. Children who have gone through a divorce have a hard time trusting anyone.

They figure, "I've been abandoned once; it may happen again. I was hurt before, and I don't want to be hurt again." Their solution? Don't let anyone inside. Build walls that are firm, strong and high, and guard them carefully. If no one can get in the castle, it will never fall. Loneliness is better than the aching pain of disappointment.

They resist change. If their lives have been harmed by change, they long for stability. They want to make sure that things aren't going to be thrown into upheaval again. This can produce a stubbornness that is quite remarkable and can bring about tremendous conflict with parents.

They can become selfish. If others have not looked out for them, then they decide they should look out for themselves. They regard other people, especially their parents, as those who are out to take something away from them. So they hold on for dear life to anything that is meaningful to them, protecting themselves unnecessarily. It is easy for them to become self-pitying when there is so much hurt in their lives.

The older they are, the more difficult it is. As I mentioned earlier, we have observed that the degree of difficulty of each child's adjustment to a divorce and remarriage increases in direct proportion to their ages. Younger children seem to be able to make adjustments easier than the older ones.

Win the Hearts of the Children

If you are the new spouse stepping into an existing family, you have your work cut out for you. In most cases, the children have had a parent that divorce or death has taken from their home. Any life situation that brings you into an existent family will require you to give plenty of love and to be very patient. You are not only marrying a spouse; you are "adopting" a family because they come as one package. Therefore, you must love and care for the children. If the children are older, then you must realize that it will require immense amounts of love and perhaps a longer period of time to win them over. And that is what you must do—win them over.

You cannot force your way into their hearts. They will have to open the door and let you in. Some stepparents may try to kick the door down. Others will bang on the door, waiting impatiently for it to open. Still others may become angry that there is a door at all, and they waste time wishing it would go away. And finally there are those who will sit out on the front steps, depressed and feeling sorry for themselves because they aren't being let inside.

Your inspiration and example must be God himself. Think about how God has reached out to you, and how he, over time, drew you to himself by a love that was greater and more patient than any love you had ever known. Think of the sacrifice he made: he gave up his only son in the hopes of winning the hearts of those who did not care about him at all. He reached out time and time again, only to be met with apathy, disrespect and hostility. In the first book of the Bible, God comes looking for Adam and Eve. "Where are you?" he asks of his children who in guilt and rebellion are hiding from him (Genesis 3:9). And the story is the same throughout the whole Bible, finally ending on the same note in the last book: "Here I am! I stand at the door and knock," says Jesus on God's behalf (Revelation 3:20). If you find yourself weary of trying to reach the heart of a stepchild, remember what God has done for you, and be chastened and inspired to never give up.

I am not saying that you should become a doormat or that you should allow yourself to be disrespected or disdained. Not at all! If you behave as if you are not worthy of respect, you will not be respected. But with loving dedication you must fully apply yourself to building a relationship with the children of your new spouse.

You cannot replace the parent they have lost. In a strange way, even if the children love you, they may be reluctant to give you their hearts because they then feel disloyal to their lost parent. The ties of children to their parents run deep. Even if children have been terribly treated by the now absent parent, they still have an almost mystical attachment to him or her. It is a grave mistake for either the divorced parent or the stepparent to try to destroy that love, or for the stepparent to try to compete with it. Give them your own love and gradually they can learn to love you both.

If you are a man marrying into a family that has older children, you must be especially patient. Realize that you cannot step in and immediately be the heavy-handed disciplinarian. You will probably see many behavior problems that need a father's firmness, but you must proceed slowly. Give the children time to know and love you before you take on that role. And understand, with some of the older kids you will never be able to treat them as if you had raised them from infancy.

Having said that, parents must still work out how the children will be disciplined. The new parent will have to have some authority. It may not be the same as if they were the biological parent, but they must have a role of respect and leadership. If the "real" parent is protective and possessive, the new parent will have a hard time being accepted. Geri and I worked with one family outside our church in which there was a rebellious son who was selfish and obstinate and gave his mother extreme difficulty. After her marriage, the new husband would try to discipline the son when he was rebellious. Even though she was being treated horribly by her son, the mother would immediately rush to his defense. Although we tried to get the husband and wife to unite to help the young man, they never really listened. The family fell apart, and the husband and wife eventually divorced.

Don't let this happen to you! Especially when there are preteens and teens involved, work to hammer out your differences in child rearing. Get competent, godly people to help you come up with wise solutions to thorny problems, and you will greatly increase the chances of having a harmonious family. When you married each other, your commitment was, and still is, to be united for life. You must therefore be committed to work for unity with your new spouse on every issue that could possibly divide you.

A composite family is formed after habits and life patterns are set. The children already have a way of going about things, and habits don't change easily. They are reinforced by memories of the way things used to be—memories that they cling to either out of love or a desire for stability.

As you come into the family, many of your personal habits and wishes will have to change to help the children maintain order and security. When older children are involved, their habits and wishes will have to change also. Parents, you will need to be the examples of the give and take that will be necessary. You will have to have many talks to work things out, and a great spirit of love and communication will have to rule in your hearts.

Spiritual Unity Is the Key

Jesus is the great unifier. He is the key to building love and harmony in a broken and blended family. If the parents are dedicated to Jesus, and the children are taught to respect and honor him also, then everyone can come together and put aside personal feelings and preferences for the sake of Christ. It is that simple. Real unity in any situation is possible only through Jesus.

Composite families need to have a regularity and focus in their home devotionals. Singing, praying and studying the Bible together are vital in order to draw everyone close beneath the fatherly love of God. As a part of your devotions, I would strongly urge you, especially when there are older children, to have regular family meetings to air out feelings. The rule is this: anybody can say anything on his or her heart, as long as it is expressed respectfully and lovingly. Once things are out on the table, work together until there is complete unity and harmony. This kind of meeting will go a long way towards forging a family unity in your home and especially toward helping the older children to feel that they genuinely belong. This kind of meeting will also require great humility on the part of the new parent...what better way to win the hearts of the children?

Jesus' last wish and prayer was for the unity of his church. He knew how difficult it would be to achieve this unity, but how glorious it would be if it were accomplished. Let this same cry for unity be your fervent and continual prayer also. Individually, with your spouse and with your family pray always that all of you may "be brought to complete unity" (John 17:23).

Sam

Have you ridden a roller coaster lately? Out of control, exhilarating, frightening, hilarious, adrenalizing...in the middle of it you say to yourself, "I must have been out of my mind to do this...can I please get off?" The front cover of our book says it all: raising preteens and teens is a wild, crazy roller-coaster ride.

We want you to read and reread this book for encouragement, direction and inspiration, not to add to your burdens or to increase your fears. Let us leave you with a few thoughts that will help as you put the book down, walk out of the room and go take your seat once again on the most thrilling roller coaster you will ever ride in your life.

1. It is scary for everybody. All parents have their fears. All of us wonder at times if our kids are going to make it. Even if other riders look placid as they takes the dips and curves, they have their moments of fear. Three of our four kids are now disciples, and we have at times wondered about each of them making it. *Will they become disciples? Can they stand up to temptation? Will they give in to peer pressure? Can they cut it in school? Who will they marry?* The trick is to not be controlled by our fears, but to instead meet them with faith. Ultimately, all we can do is set a good example, do our best, pray our hearts out, and leave our children in the hands of God, who loves them even more than we do.

2. Expect the unexpected. As parents we never know what is going to happen next. That's the essence of a roller-coaster ride: you just never know what's coming. Even when you see where the tracks are going, you don't know how it's going to feel until you get there! There are going to be lows, highs, turns, twists, thrills, chills and screams. Forget about trying to anticipate everything; just try to hang on and not bail out in the middle of the ride! And, just when you think it is going to level out, look out, you are in for a hair-raising, bone-rattling jolt!

3. We are not in control. If anything in life shows us that we don't know what is going to happen tomorrow (James 4:13-15), it is raising preteens and teens. We cannot control all that will happen *to* them and *within* them. We must, however, believe that God is in control, and that he will give us the wisdom and guidance we need to handle whatever comes their (and our) way. We must learn to control our own responses and reactions, and to listen to God and the wise counselors he has placed in our lives.

4. The ride is over before we know it. After I write these words I will get up from my desk and go to my son's Performing Arts Awards Banquet. This event is one of many that signal the end of his high school career and that begin a summer of saying good-bye. He will come home from college to visit, but life will never be the same. He will be out on his own, with others providing the daily guidance and nurture he needs to take him the rest of the way on his life's journey. Only yesterday, it seems, we dropped him off at day care. Only a few days ago we were teaching him to ride his bike; only a while ago he was in the awkward middle school years, and now, here he is, all grown up, ready to leave us. The years fly swiftly by.

Our advice to you? Get about the business of learning, growing and changing. Face up to any sins or mistakes. Repent of the sins, correct the mistakes, and get on with the business of parenting. Don't waste an hour in despair. You are still the best ones for the job. God isn't going to fire you; he just wants you to grow, learn and change.

5. Enjoy the ride. Isn't that why you got on the roller coaster to begin with? While you still have preteens or teens at home, enjoy them! Laugh with them and at them; also laugh at yourself. Do not wait for life to even out or for them to be perfect before you start having fun! Just be grateful you still have a chance to teach them, guide them, influence them and be with them. And, who knows, laughter just might be the final missing element that will help your family be what it needs to be.

The great news is that God is still in the business of working miracles. Even though it may seem that your child is beyond help, you can know that God has a plan, and that he is faithfully working it out. You could have done some things better. Perhaps you have made terrible mistakes. The worst thing you could do is give up...give up on your kid, on yourself and on your God. You have seen too many miracles to stop believing now.

About the Authors

Sam and Geri Laing for more than twenty years have worked in ministries in Florida, Georgia, Massachusetts, New York and North Carolina. They have spoken on marriage and the family throughout the United States and in other countries. They have four children—Elizabeth, David, Jonathan and Alexandra. Their older daughter, Elizabeth, married to Kevin Thompson, joined her parents to co-author *The Wonder Years*. Kevin and Elizabeth are full-time campus ministry leaders in Atlanta.

Other DPI Books by the Authors

Raising Awesome Kids in Troubled Times
by Sam and Geri

Friends and Lovers: Marriage As God Designed It by Sam and Geri

Be Still My Soul: A Practical Guide to a Deeper Relationship with God by Sam

Mighty Man of God: A Return to the Glory of Manhood by Sam

Glory Days: Real Life Answers for Teens by Elizabeth

Who Are We?

Discipleship Publications International (DPI) began publishing in 1993. We are a nonprofit Christian publisher affiliated with the International Churches of Christ, committed to publishing and distributing materials that honor God, lift up Jesus Christ and show how his message practically applies to all areas of life. We have a deep conviction that no one changes life like Jesus and that the implementation of his teaching will revolutionize any life, any marriage, any family and any singles household.

Since our beginning we have published more than 100 titles; plus we have produced a number of important, spiritual audio products. More than one million volumes have been printed, and our works have been translated into more than a dozen languages—international is not just a part of our name! Our books are shipped regularly to every inhabited continent.

To see a more detailed description of our works, find us on the World Wide Web at www.dpibooks.org. You can order books by calling 1-888-DPI-BOOK twenty-four hours a day. From outside the US, call 978-670-8840 during Boston-area business hours.

We appreciate the hundreds of comments we have received from readers. We would love to hear from you. Here are other ways to get in touch:

Mail: DPI, 2 Sterling Road, Billerica,
Massachusetts 01862
E-mail: dpibooks@icoc.org

Find Us on the World Wide Web

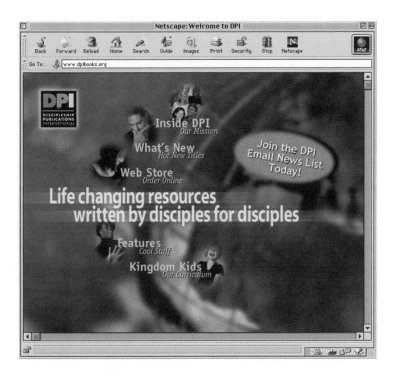

www.dpibooks.org
1-888-DPI-BOOK
outside US: 978-670-8840